How
to Be a
Cat

How to Be a Cat

Kitty Pusskin's Guide to Living with Humans and Getting the Upper Paw

As told to Mark Leigh

Michael O'Mara Books Limited

First published in Great Britain in 2016 by
Michael O'Mara Books Limited
9 Lion Yard
Tremadoc Road
London SW4 7NQ

A CIP catalogue record for this book is available from the British Library.

Papers used by Michael O'Mara Books Limited are natural, recyclable
products made from wood grown in sustainable forests. The
manufacturing processes conform to the environmental regulations of the
country of origin.

ISBN: 978-1-78243-492-4 in hardback print format
ISBN: 978-1-78243-491-7 in e-book format

1 3 5 7 9 10 8 6 4 2

Designed and typeset by Design 23

All photos from Shutterstock, apart from those of the author,
© Sophy Maudsley

Illustrations by Gillian Johnson

Printed and bound by CPI Group (UK) Ltd, Croydon, CR0 4YY

www.mombooks.com

INTRODUCTION

You're a cat. Once you get over the fact that you usually have to sleep on the floor and eat from a bowl, you'll realize it's not such a bad life. There's a lot of sleep, considerable mouse maiming and, of course, that sweet, sweet catnip. The biggest issue we have (apart from shouty dogs) is living with people. As a cat you have to realize that it's not enough merely to coexist with humans; you have to immediately adopt the position of alpha male or female of the pack. And by pack, I mean the family you live with. Dogs usually demonstrate this status by growling and being aggressive, but for cats, the keyword is subtlety. The two main ways to express our clear supremacy in the household are by ignoring any sort of command whatsoever and by adopting a look that is in equal parts pity, arrogance, ambivalence and scorn. It's what I call having the right 'catitude'.

And that's where this book comes in. Much more than simply a comprehensive A-to-Z guide, *How to Be a Cat* shows you exactly how to demonstrate this air of superiority in all aspects of your behaviour, whether it's being fickle, demonstrating a complete and utter disregard for the concept of 'blame' or constantly trying to trip people on the stairs.

These invaluable insights are drawn from my own extensive experience and also from consulting with my many four-legged pals. You can read their views and advice in 'Cat Chat', a series of personal observations dotted throughout the book.

If you're worried about how exactly a family pet can gain the upper paw over the humans, just think about your moggy heritage. The fact we were worshipped by the Ancient Egyptians, stroked by Bond villains and associated with witches makes us revered, evil and mysterious in equal measures. And if people don't respect this fierce reputation, remember this crucial piece of advice for your relationship with humans: **don't recognize them as owners; treat them as staff**.

Kitty Pusskin
Surrey, England

ALLEY CATS

Cats loitering or sleeping in alleyways aren't necessarily homeless strays or feral. They might just be hanging around these often unsavoury places to impress female cats. After all, who can resist a bad boy?

ALPHA MALES/FEMALES

One of the best things about being a cat is that the moment you enter your home, you automatically become the alpha male or female of your human family.

How? You just do.

Because being superior is genetically programmed into our feline DNA, you don't have to be aggressive, scratchy or hissy to prove who's boss. Being the alpha male or female gives you certain automatic rights:

- The right to go through all doors in front of a human
- The right to go up and down stairs in front of a human
- The right to make any warm and soft surface your bed
- The right to ignore any command

It's essential that you exercise these rights on a daily basis otherwise, as ridiculous as it seems, one of the humans might get it into their head that they're actually better than you (or at least your equal).

Of course, being alpha male or female also means **getting your own way** in any number of situations. Try this simple test to see if you're really King Kitty.

Are you the alpha male or alpha female of the family?

What do you call the main human in your household?
    A. Master or Mistress
    B. Owner
    C. That schmuck

Where do you sleep each night?
    A. On the landing
    B. On my owner's bed
    C. In my owner's bed

How do you react when your owners go out?
    A. I feel sad and lonely
    B. I sleep or play with my toys. Every now and then

I might look out of the window or wander into the street to see if they're coming home

C. They've gone out? Really? I hadn't noticed

How do you usually walk downstairs?

A. Behind my owner

B. In front of my owner

C. Any way that constitutes the maximum tripping hazard

When you see a roast-chicken dinner on the table, what do you think?

A. I hope my owners give me a morsel

B. Mine. All mine!

C. I don't bother to think. I just jump

How do you respond when your owner asks, 'Who's a good kitty?'

A. I am! I am! I am! I am!

B. It's me. I'm the good kitty!

C. You talkin' to me? You talkin' to ME?

When your owner shouts for you to 'get down', what is your immediate reaction?

A. Of course. Right away!

B. In my own good time

C. You're kidding, right?!

RESULTS

Mainly As
You're more of a pussy than a cat. Grow some! (A human figure of speech, and especially ironic if you've just been neutered.)

Mainly Bs
While not alpha status at the moment, adopting a surlier attitude, stealing food off plates and exhibiting even more ambivalence towards any command will help you grow into this role.

Mainly Cs
With that combination of self-assurance and arrogance, when it comes to exerting your authority on the household, you're definitely the Cat's Whiskers.

CAT CHAT

Bossy
Of course I rule the household. Can't you tell?

ANAL GLANDS

If you were to play a cat-themed word-association game, you might come up with descriptive words like 'sophisticated' and 'superior', perhaps also 'graceful' and 'elegant'. Words that shouldn't come to mind are 'anal glands' and 'pungent'. However, unfortunately, these too are part and parcel of feline life.

To be frank (and it's difficult not to be when discussing our bottoms), anal glands are a complete pain in the backside. To make them sound less unpleasant, your owner might call them 'scent glands' but, however you wrap them up, they're the same thing: two pea-sized sacs, one on either side of the anus containing the liquid pheromones we use to mark our territory.

Usually anal glands empty automatically when we poop and we don't need to give them a second thought. Sometimes, though, they don't drain. You'll know when this happens because your bottom will feel irritated and you'll indulge in some very unrefined behaviour, such as dragging your butt along the floor or trying to bite or scratch it. In some cases there'll also be a disgusting fishy smell coming from the area.

Whatever the indications (and for the love of catnip let's hope it's not the last one), this is an aspect of our lives where we definitely need human help. If you're fortunate, your owner will take you to the vet (one of the rare occasions I'll say that) rather than attempt the procedure themself. It's important to remember that inserting a lubricated gloved finger into your kitty anus and poking around is best left to someone who attended veterinary college. It is not a task for someone whose first thought is, 'I'll give it a go.'

ANIMAL PSYCHOLOGISTS

You may have heard your owners talking about taking you to the cat shrink. Don't worry, you're not going to some mysterious place where you go in as a fat tabby and come out as a Singapura kitten.

What they're referring to is a feline psychologist or behaviourist. This is someone your gullible owners pay lots of money to, just so they can be told that the reason you poop in their shoes is because they didn't pet you enough as a kitten.

CAT CHAT
Snickers
So the cat psychologist put me on her velvet couch for analysis. Not a good idea when the very reason I'm here is because I keep scratching the furniture …

ANKLE

This is the joint that connects a human's foot to its leg. It's very useful for them as it enables their foot to enjoy side-to-side and up-and-down movement. It's useful to us as a convenient scratching post in order to get their attention.

BABIES

The human equivalent of newborn kittens, these small creatures don't actually do much. They dribble, burble and make noises from their bottoms, yet even such limited actions are enough to threaten your position as the cutest thing in the household. That means that until the baby gets older and loses its novelty value, you have to raise your game – whether it's climbing into a vase, getting tangled in a ball of string or sleeping in the sink.

BACK-ARCHING

Thanks to our large number of vertebrae, we can raise our backs high in the air to a degree most Olympic gymnasts can only dream of. This is great for two reasons (well, three if you include 'showing off'): 1) it enables us to stretch our muscles after a deep sleep, and 2) it allows us to present a larger, more threatening profile to enemies if we think we're in danger.

There's one problem when we're at maximum elevation, though: mice running underneath us.

BANDANAS AND KERCHIEFS

These two items of kitty couture are very hard to pull off. Get them right and you'll look cool, mean and rebellious, as if you're in some sort of intimidating feline street gang like the Kitty Brotherhood or the East Side Mousers. Get it wrong and you'll look like you've got a serviette tucked into your collar. Not so much badass gang member as messy eater.

Outlaw
No one messes with the Jones Street Pussies. (Come to think of it, that's not a very good name for a tough street gang.)

BATHS

The truth is, cats don't need baths. Unlike dogs, which tend to have a laissez-faire attitude towards personal hygiene, we're usually scrupulously clean, constantly and energetically grooming ourselves for three main reasons:

A. To eliminate parasites
B. To keep our coats clean and smooth
C. To avoid baths

Some owners don't realize that even what seems like the most ingrained dirt or debris can be removed by a combination of tongue, jaws, paws and claws, and they insist on bathing us. If you detect yourself being carried towards a bath or sink, it's time to protest. I'm not talking about passive resistance like folding your paws and adopting a surly attitude; what you need to do is **struggle and lash out as violently as you can**.

What starts off as a well-intentioned attempt to get you clean should end up with you dry and your owner swearing and dabbing their scratched hands and arms with antiseptic.

CAT CHAT

Milly
This is why we hate baths.

See also *Water*

BATHROOMS

This room is very, very important to humans. Apart from containing their toilet, shower or bath, it's the one place in the house where they can be truly alone. Unless they have a cat.

Given that you're not able to let yourself in, as soon as your owner disappears into this room, meow, scratch at the door or slide your paws underneath it. They'll see it as a sign of separation anxiety and won't even contemplate that the only reason you're doing it is to spoil their 'me time'.

CAT CHAT

Moglet
Surprise!

See also *Toilets*

BEDDING, HUMAN

Sheets, quilts, blankets and duvets: to humans, this is bedding. To us, though, it's a **canvas** – the perfect place to be creative and make a statement.

Most humans unfortunately don't appreciate our art and will interpret your efforts as just a random procession of muddy pawprints rather than a fine example of abstract expressionism. Ignore their silly shouts and shooing: they are philistines who don't appreciate your message about rebellion, anarchy and nihilism and don't realize that living under their roof isn't just Mr Tibbles, but a true Pussy Pollock.

See also *Making the bed*, *Pianos* and *Toilet paper*

BEGGING

Cats shouldn't beg for anything. Not food, not mercy and definitely not forgiveness.

Do not lower yourself to the level of dogs. You're better than that.

Far, far better.

BEING CALLED

For cats, being called is the equivalent in the human world of being left a voicemail message: you don't have to respond straight away. In fact, you should actually ignore it and reply in your own good time, if ever. Reacting straight away is a sign of subservience and dependence that we've come to expect from dogs.

A DOG'S REACTION WHEN CALLED

Me? You want me? Really? Now?
I'm coming. Wait for me! I love you!

A CAT'S REACTION WHEN CALLED

What's that noise?

BEING CUTE

If you're a kitten, then take a moment away from this book and look in the mirror. You see that thing looking back at you? That's what humans know as 'cute'.

It's a concept that's hard to define; sure, there are our fluffy bodies, our oversized eyes and helpless expressions but, at the end of the day, 'cuteness' just is. And the best thing is, you don't need to work towards it. It's part of your very being and it's what humans call a 'Get Out Of Jail' card when it comes to any incidents in the house involving clawing, scratching, ripping, breaking or pooping.

You need to make the most of it, though. Cuteness fades when you're about five or six months old – the equivalent of being a human teenager.

CAT CHAT

Marshmallow
With looks like these, I can get away with murder.

BELLY-RUB TRAP

You're going about your everyday business when you're suddenly taken by the overwhelming desire to scratch something. There's your favourite tree in the garden, but it's raining; your scratching post doesn't excite you any more and the last time you used the leg of that valuable antique table ... well, let's not dwell on the unpleasant repercussions of that particular decision.

All you need to do in this situation is roll on to your back and present your belly to the nearest human. They'll take this as an open invitation to give you some tummy love. Let them do it for a few seconds, then BANG! In one fluid move, throw yourself on to your side, curl slightly and lash out with your claws!

Humans! They fall for it every time.

See also *Playing with humans*

BIRDS

On the face of it, birds make the perfect prey: they're small, they're not too crunchy, that hopping thing they do makes them slow on the ground and they attract our attention by making interesting squeaky noises. Don't be fooled, though.

They have mastered the one thing that has evaded and frustrated cats over thousands of years of evolution – the ability to leap into the air … and not come down for a while.

3 very important things every cat needs to know about birds

1. They can fly
2. You can't
3. Don't try to

CAT CHAT

Milly
A tasty snack.
So near,
yet so far …

Dexter
No comment.

BUDGERIGARS

Some owners tease us, placing small colourful domesticated birds within easy reach, yet separated from us by a secure cage. These creatures are known as budgerigars or budgies, and were put on this earth to fulfil two functions:

- To keep humans, especially small or old ones, amused
- To teach us all about frustration

BITING

Most things humans say can be completely ignored, such as 'Get down!', 'Stop it!' and 'Get off my chest. I can't breathe!' There's one thing they say, though, that should definitely be respected, and that's 'Never bite the hand that feeds you.'

There are two good reasons why:

1. Ignoring this advice will usually result in you being shouted at and/or squirted with water.
2. Worse still, biting your owner might result in them needing medical attention, with a corresponding temporary inability to provide you with dinner.

BLADDERS

Forget heart and brain. Forget even liver and pancreas. The most important human internal organ is their bladder or, as we call it, 'the alarm clock'. It's located at the base of their stomach and knowing its precise location is essential for cats. Pushing down on it or even kneading it gently with your paws will wake them from even the deepest of sleeps so they can feed you.

See also *Waking humans*

BLAME

As you'll learn from studying this book, there are many differences between cats and dogs, but one of the most fundamental is our attitude to blame. **In basic terms, dogs accept it and we don't.**

Say you're in the living room and you accidentally knock an ornament off a shelf with your tail moments before a human walks in and sees it lying shattered on the floor. Consider the two different reactions:

What a dog would do

He'd look guilty and ashamed and think, 'I'm soooooooo sorry. It was a clumsy accident and it won't happen again. I love you so much.'

What you must do

Completely ignore what's just happened and give a look that says, 'That ornament? Don't know anything about it. It's broken? Meh. Ask the dog.'

BUTTERED CAT PARADOX

Yes. You read it right.

This is yet another example of humans having too much time on their hands. After they figured out why we land on our feet (something to do with reducing the moment of inertia and the conservation of angular momentum … don't ask), they turned their attention to the adage that buttered toast always lands buttered side down. Some bright spark then thought, 'Hey. I wonder if the cat would still land on its feet if I attached some buttered toast butter side up to its back and then dropped the cat from a great height.'

As far as I know, this paradox remains theoretical but, although it might go against every instinct, when anyone comes near you with buttered toast, run far away.

It's better to be hungry than a badly bruised test subject.

See also *Nine lives* and *Schrödinger, Erwin*

BUTT-SNIFFING

Thanks to our 80 million smell receptors and a special scent sensor in the roof of our mouths, we have a sense of smell that's about fifteen times more sensitive than humans'! The advantage is that we can smell a Sunday roast from about three streets away. The disadvantage is that anything unpleasantly whiffy stinks fifteen times worse.

It's this great sense of smell that gives us all the information we need about another cat, and the process by which we gather said information is butt-sniffing. Don't worry about what others (and by others I mean your owners) think about butt-sniffing; it's perfectly normal behaviour, not some kitty deviant act. In human terms it's the equivalent of checking out another cat's Twitter feed.

The scent emitted from the other cat's anal glands tells us all about its gender, emotional state and temperament, but the truth is we don't actually have to poke our nose right under their tail. In reality, our acute sense of smell means we can pick all this information up with just a couple of whiffs from down the road.

The reason for sniffing other cats' butts is simple. It's so you can gross out your owner by rubbing your face against theirs immediately afterwards.

CAR BONNETS

It doesn't matter whether it's a Jaguar, a Ford Puma or a car without a feline-related name, when it comes to good places to sleep it's difficult to beat a car bonnet. But it's not as simple as that. There are certain rules to adhere to in order to achieve a satisfying and cosy experience.

Rule 1: For maximum comfort, choose a car bonnet that is warm.

Rule 2: For maximum safety, choose a car that is stationary.

CARDBOARD BOXES

If there's one thing guaranteed to make us smile like, well, like a Cheshire cat, it's a cardboard box. To humans they're simply empty containers that have served their purpose. To us, though, they represent the lair that our ancestors had in the wild: a secluded living space that provided shelter, security and concealment, enabling us to leap out at prey with the element of surprise. Although, nowadays, the thing you sink your claws into is less likely to be a shrew or small rodent and more likely to be a ball of wool or an ankle.

CAT CHAT

Lily
I am a natural-born killer and this is my lair.
Hey ... stop laughing!

CARS

There's only one thing cats need to know about cars: **four legs good; four wheels bad.**

Dogs have it easy: they can sit on the back seat or in

the very back of the vehicle, poke their heads out of the windows, have the wind massage their cheeks and take in the myriad exciting smells that waft by. We, on the other hand, are confined to a cramped box called a cat carrier and don't have any of these opportunities. All we can do is hunker down and get buffeted about as our owners swerve around corners and crash over bumps without any regard for our well-being. And if feeling nauseous wasn't bad enough, your eventual destination will always be a huge disappointment.

The truth about car journeys

Where you think you're going	Where you invariably end up
Holiday	Vet
Groomers	Vet
Cat show	Vet
Vet	Cattery

See also *Cat carriers*

CAT BEDS – A HANDY GUIDE

Your human family will have probably provided you with a cat bed. However, there are so many types available that it is vital that yours is suitable – and by suitable I mean comfortable and not a subject for ridicule from other cats in the neighbourhood.

This guide highlights some of the issues inherent with certain designs.

Cat cave

The word 'cave' is not synonymous with the word 'comfort', and so it is with this type of cat bed. As its name suggests, this style of bed resembles a soft cave-like structure with a relatively small opening at the front. Beware: what you gain in privacy, you lose in claustrophobia.

Cat igloo

A variation of the cat cave that delivers all the cosiness you'd associate with a real-life igloo. The manufacturers often confuse 'snug' with 'cramped'.

Wigwam cat bed

Haven't Native Americans suffered enough? The last thing this proud indigenous race needs is to see the ingenious design and structure of its traditional dwelling reduced to a pet bed. Avoid these beds out of respect.

Three-in-one bed

Not three cats in one bed. Instead, by pushing and pulling different parts, these devices convert from a cat cave, to a cat bed, to a cat couch … and perform as none of them well. (For example, the so-called couch basically turns out to be a three-sided plush-lined box.) Three times the flexibility? More like three times the discomfort.

Radiator beds

A sort of hammock-style bed that's suspended from the radiator in the mistaken belief that you'll find it all snug and homely. The reality is less bed and more sauna. Useful if you want to lose pounds as well as sleep.

Kitty cottage

I'm not sure what makes a large, plain, fur-lined cube with a hole for a door a cottage, but then again I don't work in marketing.

Cat pod

If I were leading the first cat mission to Mars I'd probably sleep in one of these. But I'm not. I live in a nice house in the suburbs and I want a bed that's described as comfortable and not 'ultra-chic', 'avant-garde' or 'trendsetting'.

Oval cat bed

Now you're talking! A standard fleece-lined (or faux sheep-skin) cat bed that promises a 'comfortable and cosy haven' whether I'm 'lounging or sleeping'. What more can a cat wish for?

The top 10 places for cats to sleep other than their cat bed

Of course, being a cat means we can sleep where we damn well want to – cat beds don't have to be actual cat beds, so sleeping anywhere in the house will do. And it's important to remember that there is an inverse relationship between comfort and where humans don't want you to sleep when you choose your nap location.

According to research I've conducted with my feline friends, the spots below are the most popular in terms of cosiness, warmth and annoyance.

- on top of a pile of clean laundry
- on top of a pile of important paperwork
- on a computer keyboard/printer/scanner
- between a computer keyboard and the screen
- directly in front of a door
- in the middle of the doorway itself
- inside an underwear drawer
- in a litter box
- on your owner's car keys (as they're frantically trying to find them)
- on your owner's head while they sleep

CAT CHAT

Blossom
A new cat bed?
Hmmm. Not quite
what I had in mind.

CAT CARRIERS

Humans call them cat carriers; we think of them as mobile prisons. You'll find yourself being dumped unceremoniously into one of them because your owner doesn't trust you loose in the car. They're worried you'll leap on to the driver's head or jump into the front, run along the top of the dashboard and poke your head through the steering wheel while the car's in motion. And, to be honest, they'd be right. Even in a small car there's a lot of space for a cat to combine exercise, fun and recklessness.

3 WAYS TO PASS THE TIME IN YOUR MINIATURE PLASTIC PRISON

- Each time a minute passes, scratch a small line on the inside of your plastic cell. This will remind you of every moment of your captivity and could be used as evidence in a future feline rights trial
- Play a haunting lament on a mouth organ. If you can't actually play the mouth organ (not having opposable thumbs puts us at a disadvantage here), then meow the tune instead
- Bang your food bowl against the bars to get attention

CAT CHAT

Simba
No bars are
gonna hold me,
man!

CAT FLAP

Forget the wheel, the light bulb and the internal combustion engine. Even forget penicillin, the internet and the Comic Sans typeface. The greatest human invention ever has got to be the cat flap.

It's hard to imagine a time before the cat flap. A time when we were reliant on humans; a time when we had to meow plaintively to be let out or in. I don't know about you, but just thinking about those dark days of dependency makes me shiver. What we had to put up with was almost criminal.

Now, thanks to this simple device, we can come and go as we darn well please. What's more, some sophisticated cat flaps only open when they detect your microchip or a small transmitter, which means any stray or unsavoury cats in the neighbourhood can't get in and steal your food or play with your favourite toy mouse containing a bell.

Of course, the downside is that, in the same way, you'll be denied access to other cats' houses and the chance to eat *their* food or play with *their* toys …

Meh. You win some; you lose some.

The acclaimed human scientist Sir Isaac Newton is said to have invented the cat flap. (Yes, I found that hard to believe, too.) When it comes down to this and laying down the Three Laws of Motion, it doesn't take a genius to know what's significantly more important.

CATNAP

As a cat, it's vital for your health and general well-being that you get enough rest. You can do this with the help of catnaps, a series of short sleeps during the day taken between longer sleeps.

CAT CHAT

Rocky
Shhhh. I'm dreaming about sleeping.

See also *Sleeping*

CATNIP

The formal name for this plant, a member of the mint family, is *Nepeta cataria.* Informally, however, it's known as the crack cocaine of the cat world. Humans like giving us catnip-infused toys and scratching posts because they can see how these things drive us wild. It's true – the substance does have a powerful effect on us, stimulating pleasure receptors in our brains and making us flip out, jump, roll about and generally get extremely excitable. As anyone who's sniffed catnip knows, the sensation is hugely enjoyable and this hyperactivity is fine while it lasts. The hard truth, though, is that **no substance takes you down faster or harder than catnip.**

THE EFFECTS OF CATNIP

Catnip speeds up your whole body. Your heart beats more quickly. You meow and purr faster. You can chase birds and your tail more effectively. You have less need for sleep (only nine hours a day). You feel happy and excited, like you've suddenly come across an unattended chicken dinner.

The consequence of this catnip high is that it's inevitably followed by the catnip crash. You'll recognize the symptoms. After all the euphoria you feel sad and tired. In many cases, you can also feel angry and nervous. It's like the anticipation of going to the vet … but much, much worse. You might also get feelings of paranoia, like that big tomcat who lives round the corner is out to get you.

The biggest consequence, however, is that you'll get a very strong craving to sniff catnip again to make you feel happy and excited once more – and the whole vicious circle starts again.

Are YOU addicted to catnip?
Take this test to find out

1. Is your catnip use interfering with your relationship with other cats or your kittens? [ ] Yes   [ ] No
2. Do you experience an anticipation high just knowing you're about to sniff catnip? [ ] Yes   [ ] No
3. Do you think those sparrows on the washing line are talking about you? [ ] Yes [ ] No
4. Do you have an uncontrollable urge to sniff catnip when you don't have it? [ ] Yes   [ ] No
5. Have you ever lied to or misled other cats about how much or how often you smell catnip? [ ] Yes [ ] No
6. Do you suffer from a chronically runny nose or frequent nosebleeds? [ ] Yes [ ] No
7. Have you tried to quit or cut down on your catnip use, only to find that you couldn't? [ ] Yes [ ] No
8. Are you nervous and restless (well, more than you are normally, given that you may share the house with a big dog)? [ ] Yes [ ] No
9. Do you spend time hanging out with cats or in places you'd normally keep clear of, but for the availability of catnip? [ ] Yes [ ] No
10. When presented with a bowl full of chicken and turkey cat food, do you sometimes think the unthinkable: 'I'm not that hungry'? [ ] Yes [ ] No

Results

If you answered YES to even one question then you might have a serious catnip addiction. The first step to getting help is admitting you have a problem, and this might take some serious soul-searching and brutal honesty.

CAT CHAT

Marlow
I got into a bad crowd and was soon freebasing catnip seven or eight times a day. Thankfully that's all behind me now and I just have an occasional sniff now and then.

See also *Catnip Anonymous*

CATNIP ANONYMOUS

A mutual-aid group, CA is open to any cat, regardless of breed (even ginger cats are welcome). The only requirement for membership is a desire to control your catnip consumption, one day at a time. Since the organization was founded in 1935, more than two million cats worldwide have found a new life outside of catnip dependency.

CAT PHILOSOPHY

It's important to adopt an ethos by which to live as early as possible. These 'cat life lessons' were created by feline philosophers far cleverer than me; in human terms they'd be the pussy Plato or the kitty Kant. Adhere to the following principles and you'll live a good and stress-free life.

3 hugely important cat life lessons

- When the going gets tough, take a nap
- If at first you don't succeed, take a nap
- If it ain't broke, take a nap

CAT SHOWS

Dogs always look uncomfortable when being groomed to within an inch of their lives and when paraded around a ring but, for cats, it feels natural; the chance to strut around and revel in the applause and cheers of spectators while being judged on your grace, charm and elegance, all the time looking haughty and self-important. I mean, why do you think they call it the catwalk?

When it comes to cat shows, there are two types: professional (for pedigrees) and amateur (for moggies).

3 signs of a professional cat show

1. The judges takes themselves sooooo seriously. I mean, they're scrutinizing cats, not judging candidates for the Nobel Prize.
2. You won't win if you behave like a cat (in other words, meowing, swishing your tail or scratching at mites).
3. Before and during the show your owners will be as highly strung as a pedigree Siamese. And just as hissy.

3 signs of an amateur cat show

1. Categories include 'Cutest Kitten' and 'Fluffiest Tail'.
2. If you pee in the ring people will laugh, not gasp.
3. Not having testicles isn't seen as a handicap (well, not as far as the judges go).

5 tips for success on the cat-show catwalk

1. Be warned, you don't just need a glossy coat; you need a thick skin. And just like human beauty contests, you'll probably be surrounded by contestants who are incredibly, well, catty.

2. Get plenty of sleep the day before. That means eighteen hours, not the usual twelve to sixteen.
3. Make sure you poop or pee *before* the show. You'll really thank me for this advice.
4. Never get yourself down because you think that haughty Birman looks overly confident or that Persian kitten looks far too cute. It's easy to be overly critical of your looks (Sphynx cats, you know what I'm talking about).
5. If a judge or another cat annoys you (face it, it's a cat show – it's going to happen), turn the other cheek. There'll be plenty of time to lash out at them after you've won.

CAT CHAT

Cupcake
My top tip for cat-show success? Remember to walk with a sassy attitude.

CATTERY

This is where you might end up when your owners are on holiday. They'll probably tell you that you're going to stay in a kitty hotel and, on the face of it, this sounds very appealing. It conjures up images of you being pampered, having access to a mini-bar stocked with treats and a retinue of staff attending to your every whim. The reality is somewhat different, the main problem being that the people who run catteries tend to confuse 'hotel' with 'detention camp', resulting in the place you end up staying at having all the luxury, charm and allure of Guantanamo Bay.

5 signs you're in a really bad cattery

1. You want to throw up as soon as you see the accommodation, and it's not due to fur balls.
2. There's a hair in your bed … and it's not one of yours.
3. There's a cat on heat in the pen opposite you and a steady stream of toms all night long.
4. You're kept awake at night by plaintive meows from down the corridor: 'Help me! Help me!'
5. You go home with more fleas than you went in with.

CAT TOWERS

Also called cat trees, these are less-than-sturdy Heath Robinson-like structures that masquerade as 'feline activity centres', containing posts, platforms and so-called perches. Perches? Owners forget that we're closely related to lions and pumas, not canaries.

Humans buy these contraptions under the complete misapprehension that we love exercising, playing and re-laxing on them. Do we? Do we hell! We'd get more enjoyment playing in a sink full of water than a cat tower.

There's a vast range available, some at quite extortionate prices. Your owners will believe that the more expensive the cat tree, the more we will enjoy it.

They are wrong. The more expensive the cat tree, the more we will enjoy ignoring it.

CAT CHAT

Milo
Cat towers …
do I look excited?

CHAIRS

There are just two rules when it comes to chairs:

1. Stroll past them in a nonchalant, 'Oh … that's a chair. I really couldn't care less about it' manner.
2. As soon as a human makes a move to sit there, suddenly leap up and take ownership.

CAT CHAT

Nutmeg
Your chair? Oh, really? Well, I don't see your name on it.

CHASING

Chasing stuff is not only instinctive, it's also fun and **so easy** to do!

How to chase something

1. Run after something really fast.
2. That's it.

What's more, there's absolutely NO pressure. You don't even have to catch whatever it is you're running after; the thrill is in the chase itself.

Good things to chase	Bad things to chase
Balls Balls of wool Mice Birds Squirrels Chihuahuas Spiders Anything smelling of catnip	Anything stationary Big dogs Your tail (you'll get a headache)

CHEWING

Chewing non-edible objects is an indication of barbarity and lack of civility, which is why you'll find this behaviour more frequently in dogs than cats. That said, cats DO chew human possessions.

Apart from kittens, who chew to ease the pain of teething, some of us chew because we're anxious, lonely, bored or just want attention. But, whatever the reason, we don't discriminate about what we put in our mouths. When the urge comes, we chew the nearest available object to us, whatever it may be. It's as simple as that.

Purr-lease! You didn't seriously believe that, did you?

Of course we decide what to chew and what not to chew! I mean, that's half the fun, isn't it? It's a decision based on this long-established formula, where *GL* is gratification level, *D* the duration of the chew, *N²* is naughtiness, and *ch* is choking hazard.

$$\frac{GL = D \times N^2}{ch}$$

For example, faced with a nice wooden chair leg or an old blanket, of course you'd go for the chair leg. Likewise, if you see your owner's brand-new expensive leather boots and a cushion both within reach, it's a no-brainer!

In most households there are a huge range of chewable objects, each with their own pros and cons.

N.B. In the following guide, please note that all Cons will probably also include being yelled at or having a water pistol fired at you.

My guide to chewable objects

House plants
Pros: Juicy with a rich texture and an ever-so-satisfying crunch.
Cons: Some plants are toxic to cats (any thoughts of satisfaction should be tempered with the chance of suffering kidney failure).

Chair legs
Pros: Satisfying crunchy sound and in some cases, the sweet

taste of varnish, the wood-protection equivalent of syrup or molasses.

Cons: None, really (however, ensure the chair leg is actually wood. Metal legs will severely diminish your satisfaction levels).

Electrical power cables

Pros: It's like you're attacking a dangerous snake: a feeling of supremacy.

Cons: It's like you're attacking a dangerous snake: a high likelihood of death.

Mobile phone charger cable

Pros: Lack of resistance.

Cons: Too easy to bite through. Any satisfaction is very short-lived.

Newspaper

Pros: Pleasing ripping sound; the opportunity to make confetti.
Cons: Newspaper is so chewable, any gratification is sadly over too soon.

Wallets

Pros: The texture and smell of leather; the satisfying gentle crunch of credit cards; the taste of paper money. What's not to like?
Cons: A high likelihood that you'll hear the words 'Bad Cat!' bellowed down your ear louder than you have ever heard them shouted before.

Books

Pros: Old books have a nice musty smell that can be enjoyed while you rip the covers off and start on the pages.
Cons: Possible paper cuts.

CAT CHAT

Katniss Everdeen
This spaghetti is a bit rubbery ...

See also *Shoes*

CHIHUAHUA

Really? REALLY? I have absolutely no idea why this type of dog actually exists. I've got one thing to say to any human who owns one reading this book: if you're going to have a dog as small as this, you might as well get a cat.

CAT CHAT

Bilbo
Chihuahua? Isn't that Mexican for 'waste of space'?

CHRISTMAS

This is a human festive period that tends to occur at the coldest time of the year, every year. You'll recognize it by a number of significant changes to the household, including a large influx of shouty children and a dangerous increase in your owners' stress levels.

Changes in the house that tell you it's Christmas

The tree
A small, decorated tree will suddenly appear in the living room. This is part of a strange human ritual, and peeing against it will be seen as blasphemy. It does, however, offer a good climbing opportunity, while the brightly wrapped gifts underneath it provide a challenge to your paper-shredding and ripping skills. (N.B. There will be a thin wire connecting lights on the tree to the wall. Don't chew this, or you will regret the consequences.)

Television
This is louder, brighter and more irritating than usual. While it is annoying in itself, what's worse is that the large number of humans who have invaded your house will fill all available seating in order to watch it, relegating you to the hard floor or hallway.

Nativity scene
A small religious tableau might appear, which depicts the story of what humans call the nativity. This is only of interest to cats because the wooden figures make perfect chew toys. Warning: be careful with the character known as Baby Jesus. Swallowing him will make the Second Coming quite painful.

Your involvement
Your owner will want to include you in the festivities. However, given your inability to join in carol-singing or wrapping gifts, this involvement will probably take the form of attaching fake reindeer antlers to your head. Show your appreciation by shaking these off a split second before they try and take a photograph.

Food

In addition to an excess of guests, you'll notice an even greater excess of food. Despite all the disconcerting changes going on around you, there are two words that can make Christmas worth looking forward to: buffet table. Practise leaping up like you've never leapt before.

CAT CHAT

Buster
How I love Christmas …

Maisey
Do I look like a freakin'
reindeer? Well, do I?

CLAWS

As a cat it's important to be aware of the four reasons why we have really sharp claws.

1. So we can climb things
2. So we can catch and hold on to prey
3. So we can fight back against predators
4. So we can quickly communicate this message to our owners: 'It's time to stop rubbing my belly'

CLIMBING FRAMES

There are two types of climbing frame. The first is the brightly coloured metal kind that can be found in large gardens and which young humans like to play on. The second type of climbing frame is superior; it's found indoors and it affords a far better grip. It's also known as your owner.

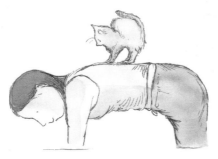

When they bend down to pick something up, leap on to their back and make your way to their shoulders. If they don't bend down then you can still reach the same vantage point by climbing up their legs. Don't be dissuaded if they're not wearing trousers – bare legs can still provide your claws with sufficient purchase.

COLLARS

There seems to be as wide a choice of cat collars as there are breeds. Most of you will have leather or fabric collars of various colours and styles that fall into three categories: the simple, the pretentious and the clichéd. In most cases your owners will make the decision for you of which collar to wear. However, be aware that there are some looks you should definitely avoid.

Avoiding fashion faux pas

Flea collars
Often it's better to put up with the irritation rather than wear a flea collar, which says more about your diminished social status than itching ever will. It's like a human wearing a replica football shirt.

Spiked or studded leather collars
Spiked collars were invented back in the day to protect domesticated cats and dogs from wolf attacks. Given the lack of wolves in today's towns and cities, the only victim you'll be is a fashion one.

Leopard-print collars
They might be our biological cousins, but wearing a leopard-print collar will only put undue pressure on you to live up to other people's (and cats') expectations. For example, your ability to swim across a watering hole or bring down a running antelope.

Pimped and personalized
Wearing a leather collar that features your name in diamanté and chrome letters can look stylish, providing your name matches the look you're trying to pull off. If you're not sure, ask yourself, 'Does my name look good spelled out in costume jewellery?' If you're called something like Capone, Gator or Beast, then the answer is probably no.

Collars featuring integrated bow ties
Seriously?

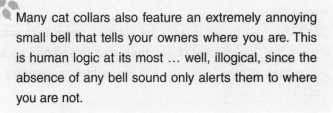

Many cat collars also feature an extremely annoying small bell that tells your owners where you are. This is human logic at its most ... well, illogical, since the absence of any bell sound only alerts them to where you are not.

Honey Boo Boo
With a name like mine, my collar
is hardly appropriate ...

COMPUTERS

It's vital that we're always the centre of attention at home, but the one thing that's an obstacle to this ambition isn't a younger, cuter cat or even a dog (heaven forbid). It's something called a computer.

This electronic device looks like a small television and it's the machine your owner spends hours each day sitting in front of, laughing at endless videos of cats – cats reacting to their reflections, cats leaping between items of furniture and missing, cats getting stuck in cardboard boxes, cats being held over the bath and shouting what sounds remarkably like 'Nooooo!'

And every minute your owner spends looking at these videos of cats is a minute they could spend playing with their real-life cat.

And that, my feline friends, is what humans call irony.

6 REASONS WHY CATS WILL NEVER EVER USE COMPUTERS

1. We get dangerously overexcited as soon as we hear the word 'mouse'.
2. And 'spam'.
3. Old habits die hard: we'd mark each website by trying to spray the screen with our scent rather than clicking on 'bookmark this page'.
4. It's impossible to download a fish.
5. Despite its misleading name, a laptop doesn't actually have a lap.
6. Carpal paw syndrome.

CAT CHAT

Teddy
If it's not a bed then why is it so warm?

Patch
The opening of my new novel:
asdfweursdhoksjkjkgnhh
hafsafsdrwwq

CURTAINS

Technically, these are pieces of cloth used to block out light or draughts, or both. To cats, they are sheer rock faces for climbing and feeding our insatiable craving for adventure. Reaching the summit (or what humans call the 'curtain pole') provides an almost incomprehensible sense of satisfaction – plus there's no chance of getting altitude sickness when you're just eight feet off the ground.

Humans think we climb curtains to give us a 'hunter's eye' view of our surroundings.

The truth is that we like the feel and the sound of our razor-sharp claws cutting into fabric. It's that simple.

CAT CHAT

Zooey
To my owner, it's a curtain. To me it's the east face of Kilimanjaro.

DINNER TIME

Better than catnip, better than that ball of wool and definitely better than chasing a bird, dinner time is the highlight of the moggy day.

In fact, there's only one thing better than dinner time, and that's two dinner times – when your owner accidentally feeds you again without realizing that someone else in the household has done the same thing. In addition, some owners will call both the meal they give you at the start of the day and the meal they give you at the end of the day 'dinner time'. Go figure.

CAT CHAT

Merlin
Well, I'm waiting …

DOGS

Like the heroic Autobots and the evil Decepticons of Transformers fame, felines and canines have been divided for centuries, locked in an endless struggle for dominance.

The reason for this hostility isn't logical. Hatred is usually based on inferiority or jealousy, but when we compare ourselves to dogs, we're so much better in every way. If you ever needed concrete proof of your superiority, just look at the list below.

10 reasons why cats are so much better than dogs

1. We have better colour vision. Dogs have trouble telling the difference between green and red. Come on, they're two completely different colours!
2. Dogs are so uncivilized. I mean, who poops in public? In the middle of the street?
3. We can be trusted to go outside whenever we want, wander around, visit friends down the street, do some sunbathing and then saunter back home for dinner and bedtime. Dogs are totally irresponsible. Let one out and at the first whiff of sausages or a fox they're off, and that's probably the last you'll ever see of them (not that I'm complaining).

4. We can hiss, just like snakes. And that makes us badass.

5. We don't, as a matter of course, have an insatiable urge to roll around in poop, decomposing animal carcasses or muddy puddles. Who would?

6. Unlike dogs, we see personal hygiene as an integral part of our daily routine and not an 'optional extra' when it comes to lifestyle choices.

7. We don't run around in circles and shout hysterically as soon as the doorbell goes. Where's the dignity in that?

8. We can see a small black mouse at the bottom of the garden on a moonless night. A dog has trouble seeing a piece of food dropped on the floor just two inches in front of its face. Idiots.

9. It doesn't really matter if a dog's name is Starey or Mr Staresworthy, if you get into a staring contest with a dog there will only ever be one winner – you.

10. Likewise, it doesn't matter if a dog can walk upright on two legs or balance a dinner plate on its nose, whatever you do, you'll always win at being cuter.

CAT CHAT

Kimmy
A dog should always know its place. In this case, as my pillow.

DOORS

Like progressive business organizations, the humans with whom you live should operate an 'open door' policy, granting you free and unhindered access to all rooms in the house. If you find any door closed, then alert your human hosts by scratching at the paint. If they fail to take notice, then clawing aggressively and damagingly at the carpet directly in front of it will soon drive the message home.

When you approach an open door with a human walking immediately behind you, don't feel pressured into actually entering. Stop in the doorway, half in and half out, projecting a 'maybe I'll go in and maybe I won't' look of indecision.

CAT CHAT

Aslan
I said I wanted access to all areas! Don't you know who I am?

DRINKS

These serve two purposes.

1. A means for humans to quench their thirst
2. Something for us to knock over for no reason

ELIZABETHAN COLLARS

This is the device that is attached to your usual collar to prevent you licking or biting at a wound or irritation. You might not know its real name, but you'll definitely recognize the indignity – the device known the world over as the Cone of Shame.

Advantages: It'll help you heal quicker.
Disadvantages: You'll look like a kitty dork.
Summary: When your ability to lick your own genitals is taken away, you'll be surprised how much free time you have.

How to maintain any semblance of self-esteem when wearing the Cone of Shame

I'm truly sorry, but there's really no way to maintain dignity by styling out what is in effect an upturned plastic lampshade. Sure, you may think that you can convince other cats that it's a special device to gather sound waves so you can hear a tin of cat food being opened from even farther away, that it's a handy way of carrying toys from room to room or even that you're waiting for it to be filled with treats … but the thing is, no one will believe you. Ever.

CAT CHAT

Macduff
I'm not pleased. My kitty pals say I look like a catellite dish.

FACEBOOKING

Not to be confused with the popular human pastime of checking social media and looking at amusing videos of cats rather than playing with an actual cat (i.e. you), facebooking is what we do to attract the attention of a human who's reading.

All you do is get between the human and the book and rub your nose and face over the pages. The human will soon get the message and put the book down in order to give you the attention you so rightly deserve.

FELINE OBESITY

Unfortunately, one of the consequences of human obesity is feline obesity. But, honestly, it's not really our fault. Our owners think that just because they like large portions and second helpings, so do we.

Actually, we do … but that's not the point. The point is that when they discover they can't finish this extra food, they give it to us and we can't say no. Look, don't beat yourself up over it: we find chicken, turkey, pork, ham, beef, tuna, salmon, eggs and cheese so, so delicious that the more we have, the more we want.

That's why all it takes is the merest whiff of a sausage sandwich and we're up on the table being shouted at.

10 SIGNS THAT YOU MAY BE A PODGY PUSSY

- You tell yourself you're just morbidly fluffy
- When humans pet you they comment that you're 'well padded'
- You only feel comfortable mating with the lights off
- You're absolutely convinced that your cat bed has somehow shrunk
- Collars with a single 'X' in the size aren't comfortable anymore
- When the vet puts you on the scales, you suck in your stomach
- You see a small bird hitching a ride on the back of a mouse just a few feet away … and you have absolutely no energy to do anything about it
- People ask you when your kittens are due … but you've been spayed
- You see yourself gaining weight in places you didn't know was possible. Fat ears? Who has those?
- Your owner changes your name from Princess Twinkle to Lardy

CAT CHAT

Alegra
Now I know where humans got the term 'Fat Cat'.

FICKLE, BEING

'Change is the only constant in life.' That was said by Heraclitus. Not the chinchilla that lives at number 13; I'm talking about the pre-Socratic Greek philosopher.

It's important for cats to demonstrate to their owners the importance of change. Not because we want to teach them about the dangers of complacency, but because it's so much fun.

Being fickle can manifest itself in many ways, but perhaps the easiest is when it comes to dinner time. At some time or another, your owners will try a new brand or flavour on you. The chances are that as long as it's a recognized cat food, you'll like it. Well, at least for the time being …

What your reaction should be after being given a brand-new flavour dinner

Day	Response
Monday	Love it
Tuesday	Love it
Wednesday	Love it
Thursday	Love it
Friday	Love it
Saturday	Love it
Sunday	Hate it

FIGURE OF EIGHT

When it comes to rubbing yourself up against humans, it's quite satisfying to drag your back, head or cheek along a single leg but, for maximum satisfaction, **you cannot beat the thrill of weaving in and out of human legs**, performing a perfect figure of eight and rubbing all your sides sequentially. Once you've mastered this skilful manoeuvre you can progress to the two advanced versions.

A. The figure of eight while the human is walking
What to watch out for: being squashed between her legs.

<u>B: The figure of eight while the</u>
<u>human is walking downstairs</u>
What to watch out for: when
you inevitably both hit the
ground, make sure the human
breaks your fall.

FIREWORKS

Believe it or not, the number-one noise that causes the greatest distress to cats isn't barking, thunder or the vacuum cleaner. It's not even Justin Bieber. It's something called fireworks.

These are small, man-made explosive devices that create noise, light and smoke. But especially noise. They were invented by humans over a thousand years ago and were believed to ward off evil spirits. Now all they do is scare pets. You'd have thought that humans would have grown tired of something that's been going on for that long, but no. They still insist on using them to celebrate events like their New Year, religious festivals, important holidays or something they call Guy Fawkes Night.

Some cat behaviourists suggest that your owner should familiarize you with fireworks by playing you a sound-effect CD, gradually increasing the volume until you become used to the loud bangs. They call this 'Sound Therapy'. I call it a high-risk strategy that will only have two possible outcomes:

1. It could acclimatize you to the noise
2. It could traumatize you even more

Don't risk the consequences. If you think your owner looks like he's going to try this experiment, drag your claws across the CD.

Dos and Don'ts for firework nights

- DO have dinner before you expect the disturbances to start, because once the fireworks begin you may be too anxious to eat*
- DO make sure you have a clear route to your designated safe haven; somewhere you can take refuge away from the noise. Whether you're a tiny kitten or an old tom, there's absolutely no shame in cowering under the couch
- DON'T wander through the cat flap into the garden when fireworks are going off. This is not the time to demonstrate bravery
- DO try and somehow convince your owner to turn on the TV as this will help to mask the noise of the fireworks. On these nights you should be thankful for the loud, screechy human talent shows that pass for light entertainment
- DON'T hiss at the fireworks. They cannot hear you and are not scared of you

*I know this sounds far-fetched, but it could happen.

See also *Thunder*

FISH

As cats, we have lots of leisure time and therefore many opportunities to ponder life's mysteries, such as why the bowl of dry food is always half empty, not half full, why humans seem to have an irrational attachment to delicate ornaments and why dogs are so dim. However, one of the things cats ponder the most is why we like fish when we clearly hate water. Some say that it goes back to our descent from wildcats, when we would eat fish if the opportunity arose. Others say that it started when the Egyptians first domesticated us by luring us into their homes with fish from the River Nile.

My view is, who the heck cares?

Tuna, salmon and sardines are so damn tasty, **and all the time you're spending wondering is time you could be spending eating.**

CAT CHAT

Missy
This will do for starters …

See also *Goldfish*

FLEAS, LICE, MITES AND TICKS

When it comes to the practice in nature of one creature acting as host for another, cats get a raw deal. Rhinos have tick-birds and sharks have remora fish to clean their teeth and eat dead skin; the connection between the different species is gratifying, harmonious and mutually beneficial.

Like dogs, we have fleas, lice, mites and ticks; not so much a symbiotic relationship as a bloody nuisance. Even our fastidious approach to grooming can't guarantee total immunity from these beastly creatures, so that's why I've created this handy guide.

Everything you need to know about pussy parasites

Fleas
While the symptoms are bad (severe itching, scratching or biting of the infected areas), what's actually worse is one specific treatment you may have to suffer. Count yourself lucky if your owner only uses drops, powder or a spray. Sometimes, though, they decide to make you wear a flea collar, a device guaranteed to kill two things stone dead: the parasites, and your reputation.

Lice
Although not as prevalent as fleas, suffering from lice is still

a social stigma worse than being seen fraternizing with the local pug. If you're forcefully cleansed with a lice shampoo then you've got off lightly. In severe cases the treatment can include having your fur shaved around the infested areas. Humans believe that baldness can be attractive or that it's a sign of virility, but a bald cat is not considered a good look under any circumstances.

Mites

Having mites makes you wish you had fleas. They're everything you don't want a parasite to be: too small to be seen by your owner's naked eye, they have tiny claws, lay eggs under the skin and are very contagious. The most common mites that cats suffer from are ear mites, which, as their name implies, make their home in our ear canals. Mites are disgusting enough, but mites that feed on earwax? You're probably feeling nauseous just reading this.

Ticks

You can get ticks if you spend lots of time walking in long grass. They're like big mites and are known as the vampire of parasites. They burrow into your skin to suck blood in the areas where you're least hairy. This means your face and neck, the insides of your legs and around your 'special place'. But apart from the danger of infection and disease, there's a far greater risk – and that's from cheapskate owners trying to save money by not buying treatments from the vet or pet shop. Instead, they might try to get rid of ticks by burning them off.

That's right. Burning them off.

Remember, if your owner holds a match or cigarette anywhere near your fur, run. As fast as you can. Being burned anywhere, particularly if it's near your undercarriage, will be far more painful than anything a tick can ever do.

CAT CHAT

Monty
I was shaved to get rid of lice. Now look at me! No one wants to be a hairless cat. Not even hairless cats.

See also *Mange*

FIVE-SECOND RULE, THE

Five seconds is the average amount of time we like to be held and cuddled. After that time you should show your displeasure by flattening your ears and wafting your tail. At this point your owners should get the hint that prolonged affection is probably not a good idea. After a further five seconds, clawing and hissing will confirm that you want to be put down more than words ever can.

See also *Human Displays of Affection (HDA)*

FOXES

These creatures really send out mixed messages. Biologically they're members of the family that includes wolves, coyotes, dingos, jackals and, of course, dogs. On the other hand, foxes have vertical pupils, can climb trees, have retractable claws, pounce on their prey and are more active at night – they actually have more in common with cats – so maybe that's why we sort of like them.

The other reason is that dogs hate foxes, and you know what they say: my enemy's enemy is my friend.

FRIDGES

There's a human book called *The Lion, the Witch and the Wardrobe* that is very relevant to cats. For a start, the lion is part of our biological family. Then there's our role as a witch's familiar. And finally, with regard to the wardrobe, we too can open the door of a large household object and enter a special, magical world. Except that in this case it's not actually a wardrobe; it's the big white thing in the kitchen called the fridge – and the world that the fridge leads to is the world of food.

It's an almost spiritual experience when your owner opens the fridge door; it'll be accompanied by a heavenly glow and the sound of feline angels meowing sweetly. Okay, I lied about the angels, but there *is* a bright light that casts a divine radiance over cooked chicken, turkey, beef, ham, tuna, salmon, sardines and a whole host of delicious treats.

The fridge will open many times during the day, usually so your owners can remove mundane items like milk, fizzy drinks or fruit juice. They see it as a chance to quench their thirst; you must see it as a chance to escape to that mystical other land.

CAT CHAT

Mr Wriggles
When the fridge door opens to reveal food, seize the opportunity ... but especially the sausages.

FULL VS EMPTY

Cats and humans have a totally different understanding of this comparison, especially when it comes to food.

<u>What humans understand by the word 'empty'</u>
Our bowl is completely devoid of food

<u>What cats understand by the word 'empty'</u>
Our bowl is less than three-quarters full

CAT CHAT

Snuggums
Yep. Looks sort of empty
to me.

FURBALLS

Just as there's no 'nice' way of talking about anal glands, there's no nice way of discussing furballs. Also known as hairballs, we can get them after licking our coat and swallowing some of the hair. Most of it comes out in our poop, but some fur accumulates in our belly and forms small wads. After a while, these get uncomfortable and you'll need to expel them by the quickest means possible: vomiting. This action will make you feel a lot, lot better, and has the added advantage that it will also really distress your owner.

To exploit this consequence, ensure that the expulsion of the furball is accompanied by what sounds like you being possessed by the demon Pazuzu from *The Exorcist* – and save it for key moments such as when your owners are just about to eat, while they're actually eating, or when they're mating.

Of course, *where* you eject your furball is just as important as *when*.

The 5 best places to vomit a furball

- Next to your owner's bed in the precise spot that she'll place her bare foot
- On an expensive rug
- In your owner's shoe
- In your owner's other shoe
- Anywhere that means she won't find it until days later

GIFTING

From what I know, human hunters tend to display their 'trophies' on plaques on the wall, in glass display cases or as rugs. We cats, on the other hand, demonstrate the results of our hunting prowess by leaving the remains of dead prey all around the house, but especially on or in our owner's possessions in order to make it easy for them to find.

Animal behaviourists say we deliver these 'treasured prizes' to humans because we consider them 'family' and want to share our kills. They call this process 'gifting' but, to be quite frank, they can call it anything they damn well like. In the end, it's one of the best ways to gross them out.

And remember, there's only one thing better than leaving a dead mouse on their bed: leaving half a dead mouse.

GINGER CATS

Unfortunately, even though we live in what we consider to be enlightened times, there is still prejudice when it comes to cat colour. If you're ginger, you'll know what I mean; the dread that comes when you trot down the street that you'll be taunted by cats meowing names at you like 'Agent Orange', 'Carrot Cat', 'Cheeseball', 'Copperknob', 'Rusty Nuts', 'UPOG' (Useless Piece of Ginge), 'Dorito', 'Mick Hucknall' and 'Prince Harry'.

If you *are* ginger, ignore this heckling and walk with your tail held high. The cats that shout these insults are just insanely jealous of your colouring, which you share with a whole host of famous and illustrious celebrity ginger cats, such as the one in *Breakfast at Tiffany's*, the one in *Alien* and … and …

Look, ginger haters, just get over it, okay?

CAT CHAT

Jaffa
I get so much abuse, so I'm grateful this photo is in black and white.

GLOW-IN-THE-DARK EYES

It won't have escaped your notice that sometimes you'll catch a glimpse of your reflection and be shocked to see you have glowing red, yellow or green eyes, making you resemble a feline fiend rather than someone cute named Fluffykins.

The truth is, you're not really possessed by some kitty demon.* This otherworldly glow is due to a special light-reflecting layer at the back of our eyeballs that makes our eyes look really creepy when viewed from a certain angle. This optical feature has two benefits:

1. It helps us see better in the dark
2. It freaks out our owners

Isn't nature wonderful?

*Well, you might be. See *Witchcraft*

See also *Staring*

GOLDFISH

Devious owners will traditionally put a whole set of obstacles in our way to prevent us reaching the creature. For example:

- It's in a potentially dangerous glass container
- It's filled with water, which we have an aversion to
- It's usually on a high shelf out of our reach (as if!)

What they fail to understand is that the repetitive motion of the goldfish and their little shimmering bodies attracts our attention like nothing else, after which a mix of curiosity, instinct and disregard for consequences kick in and nothing will stand in our way of reaching the bowl or tank.

The three stages of a goldfish encounter
- Interest
- Entertainment
- Fish dinner

CAT CHAT

Tigger
You can swim, but
you can't hide …

See also *Fish*

GRASS, EATING

As cats, we act instinctively. People, on the other hand, really overthink. A great example is how they try to figure out why, since we're predominantly carnivores, we love nibbling at grass or other vegetation – especially since we don't have the necessary enzymes in our belly to break it down. Humans have pondered this issue for years and still don't really know the answer.

Why humans think we eat grass
- It's a natural remedy for upset stomachs: the grass

makes us vomit up anything disagreeable like small bird bones or feathers
- It gives us extra nutrients and fibre
- It's a natural laxative
- It compensates for a dietary deficiency
- It's a throwback to when we scavenged in the wild
- It's a sign of anxiety

Why we really eat grass
- We like the taste

GROOMING SALONS

These places might have cute names like The Beauty Pawlour, Moggy Makeover or Groomingdales, but they only conceal the fact that behind their attractive facades are some of the most terrifying places a cat can find itself.

Don't be deceived or get lulled into a false sense of security when you get there. There'll be a nice little reception area with water and a tempting bowl of dry snacks, and it will seem like you're checking into a swish boutique cat hotel. However, the next thing you know your owner is handing you over to a complete stranger and you're taken into a room full of terrifying-looking equipment. It's like some sort of medieval torture chamber, but instead of racks, iron maidens and pliers you'll be exposed to clippers, de-matting combs and blaster-dryers.

You'll be muzzled, shackled to a rail and then sheared, shaved, cropped, clipped, trimmed and brushed to within an inch of your life – and then placed in a cage to await collection.

And if that's not warning enough to be more thorough when it comes to self-grooming, then I don't know what is!

CAT CHAT

Blossom

A lion cut? A LION CUT? And how exactly is this going to help my self-esteem?

See also *Self-grooming*

HIDING PLACES

I pity you if you live in a minimalist house – somewhere that is all white walls, distressed floorboards and voile curtains – the sort of place more suited to the lifestyle of a monk than a family of four. What minimalism means to your owners is a more organized home, more freedom and more space; the downside to you is that it means fewer places to hide.

But hiding isn't just about somewhere to go to escape

danger; it's about having a base where we can relax if we're ever feeling insecure. Not having a hiding place can make us stressed and when that happens we need to find somewhere to calm us, but if we know we don't have a hiding place we get more stressed … Look, you can see where this is going, can't you?

The top 10 reasons cats need hiding places

- A refuge from the family dog
- And small children
- And the vacuum cleaner
- Somewhere to keep cool
- Or warm
- Somewhere to sleep where our owners can't see us and moan about how long we're sleeping
- A place to go and ponder issues like, 'This family don't adequately cater for my needs. Shall I leave them for that nicer house two streets away with more hiding places?'
- Squeezing into a small space makes us feel sooooo cozy
- Somewhere to take a half-dead mouse or bird
- Fireworks

Good and bad places to hide

GOOD

- In or behind a laundry basket
- Under a radiator
- Behind curtains
- At the back of a wardrobe
- On top of a wardrobe
- Under a bed or duvet
- In a sock drawer

BAD

- Inside washing machines, dryers, dishwashers, fridges – any big white thing in the kitchen, really
- Under a car
- Under a big dog

See also *Washing machines*

HISSING

Many of the noises that animals make can be misconstrued. Fortunately for us, hissing is not one of them. That sound only means one thing: p*ss off.

There are two main questions cats tend to have about hissing, which I've answered and given a little of bit of advice on below.

I like hissing. It makes me feel important. Can I do it all the time?

You can but, like humans and their swearing, if you do it too often it loses its impact. Save hissing for when you really want to make a point. That point will usually be something like, 'Get away from me or I'll claw you.'

Sometimes I hiss but still get ignored. What am I doing wrong?

Well, presuming you're making the correct noise (it should sound like air rapidly escaping from a car tyre; that, or a pit of snakes), you're probably not accompanying it with the appropriate gestures. Performing at least two of the following actions will emphasize how you're feeling:

- widening your mouth
- arching your back
- twitching your tail
- flattening your ears
- spitting

CAT CHAT

Kipper
Am I happy, sad, playful, curious or angry? Thankfully, hissing removes the guesswork.

HUMAN DISPLAYS OF AFFECTION (HDA)

Don't let any human think they can pet you whenever they want. Sure, you might really like it when you sit on the couch next to them, but giving in too easily lets them think you need it and, as 'supplier of petting', this gives them a dominant role in the human–cat relationship. As a cat, you must choose the time and place you want affection, and make it known by resisting or even hissing so they know that now is not the right time.

Remember, **head-rubbing, back-stroking and tummy-tickling must only be done on your terms**.

See also *Five Second Rule, The*

HUMANS, OLD

These are humans that are about ten or more in our years. Having one of them as your owner can bring mixed blessings.

Advantage
They really spoil us

Disadvantage
They really fart … and we get the blame

HUMANS, YOUNG

Also known as children, these creatures are the human equivalent of kittens. Sharing a house with them has its downsides, but there's one major benefit.

Disadvantages
- They hug us too tightly
- They pet us when we're trying to eat
- They stroke our fur THE WRONG WAY!
- They pull our tails
- They hiss and meow back at us, loudly
- They play with our toys
- They sit in OUR warm spot
- They try to sit on our backs and yell, 'Horsey! Horsey!'

Advantage
- You won't go hungry: they have poor hand–eye coordination and often drop food on the floor

INDEPENDENCE

Cats might be many things – supercilious, self-important, arrogant, even – but one thing we are definitely not is needy. We're our own person. Or rather, cat. The only thing we're dependent on humans for is food. (Well, that and booster injections, but the less said about those, the better.) Thanks to the invention of the cat flap, we come and go as we please, we're self-grooming and we don't feel the need to wait by the door or the window so we can smother our owners with excessive amounts of affection the nanosecond they get home.

You know that film, *The Incredible Journey*, where a Siamese cat, a Labrador and a bull terrier travelled across 250 miles of Canadian wilderness to get back home? Well, the cat could have easily done it all on his own. The dogs were only added after test screenings to widen the film's demographic.

INOCULATIONS

Feline infectious enteritis, feline chlamydophilosis, feline leu-kaemia virus – I'm not sure what's worse, the sound of these diseases or their effects.

Fortunately for us, advances in medical science mean that our catching them can be prevented. Unfortunately, the way we're prevented from catching them is by a vet using a piece of equipment called a syringe. This syringe contains what humans call a vaccine. This is good. The syringe also contains a very pointy needle. This is very bad.

KISSING

Humans think that when we nuzzle our mouths and noses against their faces, it's the equivalent of a kiss. Fools!

We only do it because they usually have remnants of something appetizing around their mouths. It could be anything from gravy to goujons, ketchup to kippers. As long as they continue to think it's a sign of affection rather than us just wanting to try that tempting residue of spearmint toothpaste, you'll continue to receive treats.

Don't stop them believing.

CAT CHAT

Apricot
It's not love. It's that bit of bacon fat on your chin.

LAPS

No matter what breed you are (well, as long as you're not too chubby), it's almost certain that you're small enough to curl up in your owner's lap and enjoy the warmth and security of this comfortable location. What's imperative, though, is that you use all of your feline instincts to decide the optimum time to jump up and sit there.

This is always five seconds before your owner wants to get up.

LASER POINTERS

All it takes is a cheap laser pen and a flat surface and in next to no time you will be mesmerized by a dancing red dot, leaping from paw to paw and chasing it all round the room and up the curtains.

Since their invention in the late 1950s, lasers have impacted many areas of human life: astronomy, manufacturing, entertainment, medicine, warfare, consumer electronics – and now, it seems, tormenting cats.

LION KING POSE, BEING HELD IN THE

Disney has a lot to answer for. I'm not talking about the way cats have been stereotyped in various films – those creepy Siamese cats in *Lady and the Tramp* or the streetwise alley cat in *The Aristocats* – that's art imitating life. No, the most evil crime they've foisted on us is *The Lion King*.

Humans can't seem to distinguish between domestic cats and lions, and seem to find a great source of humour in holding us up high in the air and badly singing 'The Circle of Life'.

Be on your guard if anyone in your household calls you Simba or starts singing in Zulu. Or both.

LITTER TRAYS/LITTER BOXES

Pooping in public? Please, we're not barbarians.

Unlike dogs, who think everything outside the front door is a toilet, we use a tray filled with a sort of granular material that absorbs not only our pee and poop, but the smell of our pee and poop, too. This is all well and good and, providing we use it in the way it's intended, the tray maintains harmony between us and humans. However, not all litter trays are created equal.

The quality and feel of the 'litter' can vary considerably – from something that resembles fine sawdust to a substance that looks and feels like (and probably is) pieces of coal. What your owner doesn't appreciate is that you have to sit in the tray. If you feel that the litter is too coarse or lumpy, paw the offending material out on to the floor and poop next to it. It's amazing how quickly humans learn.

Stinking outside the box: the Dos and Don'ts of litter trays

- DON'T confuse a litter box with a letter box. This will result in you being shouted at
- DON'T think that a child's sandpit is a giant litter tray. Doing so will have the same effect as the above
- DO make sure the litter tray is orientated correctly within the room. There is such as thing as Feline Feng Shui and too much negative energy can prevent you pooping
- DO pretend that you're at the beach. It makes pooping much more fun
- DO make sure no one is looking. Relieving yourself should not be a spectator sport
- DON'T decide to mix it up a little and use the sink as an alternative to the litter tray. Believe me, you don't want to do this

CAT CHAT

Minka
Hey! A little privacy,
please.

See also *Toilets*

LYING ON THINGS

It's been said that if you put a piece of paper in the middle of
a football stadium, a cat would go and lie on it. While that's
a bit of an exaggeration (and anyway, what would a cat be
doing in a football stadium? We hate organized sports), there
is a kernel of truth in it. Books, newspapers, important letters,
towels, computer keyboards, car keys, items of clothing –
you name it and you've probably lain on it while your owner
is either looking for it or trying to use it.

Animal psychologists think we do this because we're
seeking attention from our owners. The simple truth is that
we do it because we know it annoys them.

Hector
And I'm annoying
you how?

MAKING THE BED

You may not know this phrase, but you'll recognize the action; it's the day when your owner takes off the old sheets, quilts, blankets or duvet and replaces them with new ones.

It should also be the day that you decide to frustrate them by getting under the covers.

MANGE

When it comes to this embarrassing skin condition caused by mites, you should hope for two things:

1. Your owners get you treated as soon as possible.
2. They only refer to it as mange and not its alternative, and far more reputation-damaging name, *scabies*.

See also *Fleas, lice, mites and ticks*

MARKING YOUR TERRITORY

Like dogs, it's a straightforward process when it comes to staking a claim as to what constitutes our territory. All you have to do to designate a space as 'yours' is just spray urine on it. It's easy. Piss-easy, in fact. This spraying isn't as prevalent after neutering (and it's usually a male thing anyway), but the signature scent of your pee means other cats in the neighbourhood immediately know that area is yours. That bit of the garden from the patio to the large rose bush? Just raise your tail and spray. That area from the end of the driveway to the lamp post? Just raise your tail and spray.

There are only two limiting factors to how much territory you can have. The first is your imagination and the second is the capacity of your bladder.

FURNITURE AS TERRITORY

Your territory doesn't have to be space outside your house. It can be your favourite chair, sofa, or your owner's bed, which you lie on when no one's home. In these cases it's not advisable to spray furniture to mark your space. Instead, rubbing your forehead, cheeks and chin against the fabric will transfer your natural scent. Your owners will appreciate this method far more.

See also *Territory*

MATING

If you're not sure what to do, I have two words of advice: don't worry.

When the time arrives, as a cat you'll find the act comes naturally and, compared to the way humans mate, it's completely without complications.

A typical human mating ritual involves	A typical feline mating ritual involves
Alcohol Fumbling Disappointment Embarrassment Regrets Recriminations Angry texts	The female presenting her raised hindquarters Er … that's it

MEOWING

When it comes to communicating with humans, it's vital that they understand the nuances of the feline language. That means educating them so they can correctly understand not only what we mean by a meow or a howl, but also pick up on changes in pitch and tempo. It's a big ask for humans to get to grips with such subtleties, so being consistent in how we talk is the best way to help them to learn what we're telling them.

There's a lot to remember, which is why I've written these notes on communication between the species.

Know your meow from your howl: My handy guide to cat communication

Sound	When you might use it	Examples of what it means in human terms
Purr	When you're content but want to convey ambivalence rather than satisfaction	Meh …
Meow (mid-pitch)	General-purpose sound used when you want something	Give me food/Let me out/Let me in/Give me more food
Chirps and chirrups (short higher-pitched sounds somewhere between a purr and a meow)	When you want to attract attention	Look at me! Look at me! Look at me! Look at me! I mean look at me now – not in five seconds!
Trill	When you're curious about something	Huh?

Crying like a human baby	When you want something or someone	FFS! Come here!
Caterwaul (a series of short, sharp yowls)	When you're in heat and want to attract males	Hey, sexy! If I said you had nice fur, would you hold it against me?
Meow (low pitch)	When you're unhappy or have a grievance	What's with that new flaked tuna crap?! Get it out of my sight RIGHT NOW!
Meow (high pitch)	When you're in sudden pain	GET OFF MY TAIL, YOU IDIOT!
Meowwww! (A long drawn-out meow)	When you're annoyed or object to something	WTF?
Growl	When you're defending your territory	Get off my land!
Hiss	When you're about to deliver a serious paw swat or a vicious nip	Come on then, if you think you're hard enough!
Wail	When you're really frightened	Damn that Dyson!
Howl	When you're feeling stressed, confused or afraid	HELLLLLLLLLLLLP!

IMPORTANT: BE PREPARED FOR THIS REACTION WHENEVER YOU MAKE A SOUND

You: Meow … Meow … Meow … Meow.
Human: Yes. Yes, I know … I know …

MICE

These small rodents combine the two things cats like best – toys and food – in one small, convenient package. From protecting grain stores back in the day to Tom and Jerry and Itchy and Scratchy, cat and mouse have fought like, well, cat and mouse. As an essential part of the feline ecosystem, there are three reasons why we catch mice, knock them from side to side with our paws and then, when we feel like it, eventually kill them:

1. For sport
2. For food
3. Because we can

Mice hunting: FAQs

Are mice really that easy to kill?
Being small and unable to fly, on the face of it mice seem like easy prey, but remember that a cornered mouse has nothing to lose (apart from its life), so it can be very vicious. For such little creatures they have very sharp claws, and those big front teeth can really hurt. What I'm saying is never underestimate your enemy (I'm not saying respect your enemy, because they're only mice … You know what I mean).

Do I have to play with the mouse before killing it?
Yes. It's important to knock the mouse about to exhaust it before going in for the kill. Failure to do this successfully

means it'll be at its strongest and more likely to fight back or, worse still, escape. And no one wants the shame and infamy of letting a cornered mouse escape. Let that happen and you'll forever be known as THAT cat.

Do I need to eat the mouse after I've killed it?
Not at all. Often the satisfaction is the thrill of the chase, and eating mouse flesh is the icing on the cake. Except it's obviously not a cake; it's a dead rodent.

Is it good manners to leave a dead mouse on my owner's doorstep?
Yes. But it's even better if you leave it under or on their bed. Or better still, in it.

Should I eat the tail? I've heard it's like spaghetti.
You heard wrong.

CAT CHAT

Smokie
Cats and mice?
It's a dog-eat-dog
world ...

See also *Gifting*

MICROCHIPS

Many of you will have had these implanted under your skin when you were a kitten. And by implanted I mean having a large needle inserted under the skin between your shoulder blades. Once fitted, you just forget it. The benefit is that if you're ever found wandering, an animal shelter or vet can scan you and reunite you with your owner. The downside is that it's impossible to be the feline equivalent of Jason Bourne and go off the grid.

You win some, you lose some.

MIDNIGHT RUNS

It's midnight. Everyone in the house is fast asleep, while outside the only sound is the gentle stirring of leaves from a soft night breeze. There's only one thing to do: **run from one end of the house to the other as fast as you can, making as much noise as possible**.

Humans hate us for this, but at the end of the day (literally) it's actually their fault. Being domesticated means we can sleep for most of the day, safe in the knowledge that when we're lying on the couch it's highly unlikely we'll be attacked by hawks or foxes. The result is that when your owner is fast asleep, you're wide awake and full of beans – and running around like a moggy madman is a good way of working off this excess energy. And when I say 'good', I mean 'annoyingly disruptive'.

10 things to do during the midnight run

1. Run from the back door to the front door. And back again
2. Repeat 1
3. Jump up on to the kitchen counter
4. Knock jars and bottles on to the floor
5. Jump down again
6. Run into the hallway, pouncing on absolutely nothing
7. Run from the front door to the back door
8. Repeat 6
9. Repeat 7
10. Repeat 6

CAT CHAT

Faustus
I'm in the zone for my midnight run. Can't you tell?

NAMES

When it comes to names, humans insist on giving us moggy monikers that fall into one of five categories.

1. Generic nice
2. Appearance-related
3. Overly noble
4. Humorous tributes to the famous (in their eyes)
5. Just plain odd

There's no issue if your name accurately sums up your character, appearance or pedigree, like Smiley, Fluff or Randolph. The problem comes when you're given a name that your owner thinks is really funny or cute and it's plainly not.

So what can a cat do? Sadly, not a lot. Sure, you can point-blank refuse to respond to that name, but that's likely to severely limit your supply of treats and catnip-infused toys. The only alternative is to learn to accept it. Unfortunately for us, as the saying goes, 'You can choose where you pee, but you can't choose your name.'

Examples of the 5 types of cat names bestowed by humans

Generic nice	Appearance-related	Overly noble	Humorous tributes to the famous	Just plain odd
Summer, Cupcake, Ziggy, Bella, Molly, Jasper, Angel, Sammy, Rocky, Pumpkin, Tucker, Jake, Felix, Scooter, Bandit, Lucky	Smokey, Tabitha, Amber, Mittens, Socks, Cocoa, Gravy, Ace, Snowy, Cinnamon, Misty, Fluff, Garfield	Lord Meowington-Hairball, Lady Boo Boo von Furrycoat, Sir Purringly-Flufftail II	Cat Stevens, J. K. Meowling, Cindy Clawford, Lionel Itchy, Olivia Mewton John, Mariah Hairy, Charles Lickens, The Great Catsby	Brian, Dave, Terence

CAT CHAT

Martin

I absolutely hate my name. Martin should be a plasterer or someone who installs fitted kitchens, not a pedigree Russian Blue.

Chairman Meow

Yes, I've got a stupid name, but in the end I don't really care what I'm called, as long as I'm called for dinner.

NEEDY OWNERS

Being highly independent creatures, we love our own space. Some humans, however, especially single females over thirty-five, form an uncomfortably close bond with us. Sure, it's great to have lots of belly-rubs, hugs, strokes and petting, but after a while you're likely to feel smothered by this affection. Literally. That's why it's probably time to make yourself scarce the moment you hear one of the following phrases.

Things owners say that indicate they're needy

- You understand me so well, it's like you can read my mind
- Who needs a boyfriend when I have you?
- I wuv you! *(said in a baby voice)*
- I dreamt about you last night
- I can't imagine life without you

Things owners say that indicate they're extremely needy

- Let's run away together and get married

NEUTERING

This section is for male cats. Females should see *Spaying*.

'Neutered'. It sounds so innocuous. It's like the word 'neutral' – you know, uninvolved or indifferent. In reality, though, nothing could be further from the truth. When you find out that the process means removing your testicles (yes, both of them), you won't be uninvolved and you definitely won't be indifferent!

The procedure has its upsides. It means you won't father any unwanted kittens and it also helps prevent cancer and prostate problems. The downside is that the operation involves something sharp and pointy in the vicinity of your genital area. If I tell you any more, you'll run away from home.

One other aspect of neutering that is even more troubling

If having someone interfere with your undercarriage without you signing a consent form isn't upsetting enough, then consider this: to stop you licking the wound you'll probably have to wear the Cone of Shame. This is often more distressing than undergoing the whole neutering procedure.

What to do after the operation
1. Have plenty of rest.
2. Practise an expression that combines these four emotions simultaneously: resignation, bitterness, anger

and resentment. This will guilt your owners into giving you extra affection but, more importantly, extra treats.

3. Carry on with 2 for as long as you can; at least until it dawns on your owner that by now you're probably faking it.

CAT CHAT

Rufus
Yes, I've just been neutered. Was it my smile that gave it away?

NINE LIVES

Like most calculations, there is an element of statistical error here. In this case, however, the figure is out by a factor of nine.

The whole idea of us having nine lives is said to be an old wives' tale, although there's a rumour it was misinformation started by dogs to instil us with a false sense of self-confidence and a penchant for recklessness. It's true that when we fall we land on our feet, yet this is not an indication of an innate ability to cheat death; it's just what humans call our 'righting reflex'. Likewise, our flexibility, good balance and ability to leap long distances mean that, although we can often escape peril, it doesn't mean we're immortal.

Dwelling on that important point is the *only time* a cat needs to be humble.

CAT CHAT

Bobo
Me, worried? Nah! I always land on my feet.

See also *Buttered Cat Paradox*

ONE-STEP RULE, THE

This should come as naturally to you as staring someone out or sleeping for 75 per cent of the day. If you don't already do this, then you need to learn immediately. The one-step rule is a staple of the human–cat relationship and is very simple to learn and practise. When you accompany humans around the house, **make sure you walk just one annoying step in front of them**.

Especially going downstairs.

See also *Stairs*

ORNAMENT ICE HOCKEY

One of the best cat games. Ever. And what's even better is that you don't need to play on ice, which is slippery and cold. You also don't need to bother yourself with boring things like defensive zones, offsides or double minor penalties. All you need to remember is that in this version of the game, the ornament is the puck and the ice rink is any smooth surface, like a tabletop, mantelpiece or shelf.

The object of the game
Use your paws to knock the ornament from side to side from one end of the playing surface to the other. Then on to the floor.

The rules
Don't get seen (okay, this isn't really a rule; it's advice).

PENS

There is a human expression, 'The pen is mightier than the sword.' That might be true in some cases, but it's definitely not mightier than the paw. When a human grasps a pen, you have to seize the opportunity: the opportunity to fight with it and even knock it out of their grip. Doing this for even a short time will remind your owner why they usually type or text everything.

CAT CHAT

Harry
I know what you're thinking: 'Shall I pick up the pen and start writing?' Well, you've gotta ask yourself one question: 'Do I feel lucky?' Well do ya, punk?

PET CAMS

Animal champion George Orwell would have had kittens if he'd lived to see these miniature cameras, sometimes containing microphones, being used to keep tabs on our every move. Owners place these devices strategically around the house so they can keep an eye on us when they're out – mainly in the mistaken belief (or rather, hope) that they'll log in one day and see us wearing clothes and prancing around on two legs.

Pet cams are usually located on a high shelf or mantelpiece, pointing towards the couch, our bed or a favourite chair. The best way to deal with them is not to climb up and knock them down (although admittedly, that is quite satisfying in its own right); instead you should exploit their presence by making sure you act up whenever your owners are watching. (You can tell because the camera light will glow.)

How to cause anxiety in your owners when you know you're on camera

A. Lie on your back with your legs in the air and hold your breath so it looks like you've gone to that great cattery in the sky.

B. Squat, and spread your hind legs so it looks like you're peeing.

C. Face away from the camera, make gagging noises and pretend to cough up a really matted sticky furball.

D. Show your owners that even a flat vertical surface like the wallpaper in the newly decorated living room is your territory. Back up to the wall, raise your tail and hindquarters and pretend to spray it.

E. Back up to the camera and position your 'special place' right in front of the lens. Stay there until your owner gets fed up or feels nauseous, whatever happens first.

PIANOS

In addition to leaving muddy paw prints on clean bedding or scratching patterns in wooden table legs, walking up and down a piano keyboard is another way we can express ourselves creatively. Just as Johann Sebastian Bach wasn't appreciated as a composer in his lifetime, humans don't really appreciate that we're creating a considered musical composition. They think that all we're doing is pressing down on random keys and creating a confused and harsh mingling of notes. They're obviously mistaking us for Girls Aloud.

CAT CHAT

Micetro
A three-octave drop in one bar? Really? Not easy when you've got a reach of just eight inches!

See also *Bedding, Human* and *Toilet paper*

PLANTS

Humans get very upset and annoyed when we claw, cleave, shred, fray, tear, rip or eat their precious plants, forgetting the fundamental rule of the feline–vegetation relationship: **A house may have a cat or plants. But not both**.

CAT CHAT

Jimbo
It was like this when I got here.

PLAYING THE CELLO

This is cat slang for the act of positioning a hind leg high behind your head and licking your 'special place' in full view of your owners or, better, their guests. To maximize their embarrassment and discomfort, it's best to 'play the cello' when they are in the company of:

    A. a potential partner

B. their in-laws

C. their boss

D. a religious leader

N.B. This position is also known as providing 'dinner and a show'.

CAT CHAT

Pixie
Playing the cello? Well, I am a mewsician.

PLAYING WITH HUMANS

Whether it's moving that felt mouse provocatively in front of you, holding you upright and trying to make you walk on two legs or using your paw to stroke their own face, humans forget that every single attempt to play with you will only end in one of three ways:

- Them being bitten
- Them being scratched
- Both of the above

No matter how many times they begin some form of playtime with us, they never seem to learn the adage, **'No game, no pain'**.

CAT CHAT

Jasper
You can rub my tummy, but only five times. Then I'll scratch.

See also *Belly-rub trap*

POOP, BURYING

If you ever needed an example of how and why we're far more civilized than our canine compatriots, then you don't need to go further than this: **dogs bury their bones; cats bury their poop**.

But it's not just about being cleaner or even demonstrating basic politeness. It's about being far more enlightened and cultivated. And if you think dogs are uncivilized for not covering up their poop afterwards, what about when they do poop and then use the kerb or a grass verge as toilet paper?

It's beyond belief. They're not animals; they're savages.

See also *Litter trays/Litter boxes*

RABIES

'The R word', 'The Big R', 'Moggy Madness' … Many cats these days are still scared of rabies, mainly out of ignorance. Although the disease has been virtually eradicated in developed countries, many myths about it persist. Myths such as, 'You can catch it from sharing another cat's bowl' or 'I'm a ginger tom so I can't catch it,' so I thought I'd better set the record straight.

The truth about rabies

- You can only catch rabies by being bitten by a mammal carrying the virus. Being playfully nipped by a wayward kitten in the house should just be seen as annoying or embarrassing rather than an automatic death sentence
- Excessive excitability is not an automatic sign that you have rabies. It could be because your owner has decided to take up knitting
- Likewise, foaming at the mouth might not signify infection.

It might just be because you've exercised a little too much, have an upset stomach or chewed a tube of toothpaste

- Anyone can be susceptible to rabies, irrespective of their breeding. Just because you're called Tatiana Fairy Dust Gorgeous-Honeybun and have been a Supreme Cat Show 'Best in Show' doesn't make you immune
- Biting someone without warning doesn't necessarily mean you've developed rabies. It could just mean that you're very naughty

3 THINGS YOU NEED TO KNOW ABOUT RABIES

- It's a virus that affects your brain and central nervous system
- It's usually fatal
- You really don't want to catch it

RAIN

This is water that falls from the sky and makes us damp and annoyed. Sometimes you go outside the back door and it's raining, so you make your way through the house to the front door only to discover that it's raining there too. **This is your owner's fault**.

RUBBING

When it comes to rubbing our body, face or paws against humans, make sure you respect what's known as the Inverse Fur–Clothing Principle. This simply states that for maximum annoyance, dark-haired cats should only rub against humans wearing light-coloured clothing, and vice versa.

SCHRÖDINGER, ERWIN

Schrödinger is best known as a quantum physicist, but he was also something else: a bad man. A very bad man, in fact. Take it from me, nothing good can ever come out of a cat being locked in a box containing a flask of poison, a radioactive source and a Geiger counter.

If you're ever approached by a scientist, just remember that the 'Schrödinger's Cat' experiment is not a paradox. It's a reason to call animal welfare. Any situation where you are simultaneously alive and dead will never end well.

SCOLDED, BEING

Clawing furniture, bringing half-dead birds into the house, jumping up on tables, knocking ornaments on to the ground … it never ceases to amaze me how humans get upset by this sort of behaviour. We're cats. It's what we do. What I'm trying to say is: be prepared to be shouted at by your owners. When this happens, you must react in the following way.

Step 1: Scamper away
Step 2: Stop after about six feet and turn to face them
Step 3: Stare

They hate that.

SCRATCHING POST

There's a good chance you've already got one of these in your house: a short, thick pole on a sturdy base, covered in a rough-textured material. What your owner is trying to tell you is that you'll get just as much satisfaction from sharpening your claws on a bit of old carpet or rough string as on the leg of a chair or the side of a sofa.

They are lying.

CAT CHAT

Mikey
Scratching post.
Chair. Meh.
Same difference.

SECOND HOMES

Unlike humans who sometimes have a second home in Florida, Provence or the Costa del Sol, our second homes are usually much closer to, well, home. They can be around the corner, on the same street or even two doors away. Essentially, these are warm places we can visit while our owners are at work. Places where we're made to feel welcome but, more importantly, places where we are offered extra meals. And what's even better is that, for a cat, there's no limit to how many second homes you can have.

Four breakfasts, anyone?

SELF-GROOMING: FAQS

Don't worry if you find yourself spending a third of your day self-grooming. It's natural and doesn't mean you suffer from obsessive-compulsive disorder. It just means you take personal hygiene and good health seriously. Remember, if *you've* noticed you're starting to smell like a damp dog, then other cats have too.

Should I have a set routine for self-grooming?
Not necessarily – sometimes it's good to mix it up a little bit. You know, one day lick your shoulders, forelegs, hind legs, flanks, tail and genitals – then the next start with your flanks, then go on to your hind legs, tail, genitals, forelegs and shoulders. Or you could start with your tail. Variety is the spice of life!

I'm an old tom and am worried that excessive grooming is a bit, well, effeminate.
There used to be a time when a male cat that spent too

long grooming himself was met with a level of scorn, derision, name-calling and sometimes bullying. Thankfully in these enlightened times it's now acceptable for male cats to spend as much care and attention grooming themselves as females.

Is it true that a dishevelled and unkempt cat is probably a sick cat?

Maybe. Or it could just mean that they're a slob.

I've got a very furry back and am worried that it's a turn-off for female cats. Should I rub it against a tree to thin it out a bit?

No. You're a cat. Cats have fur all over them and it won't affect your chances of mating. Get over it.

SEPARATION ANXIETY

Having your owner disappear from the household for a period of time is a natural part of the cat–owner relationship. They could be gone for a few minutes (they're most likely sitting on the toilet) to a few days (they're most likely sitting on a sun-lounger).

Animal psychologists have long pondered if cats are affected by what they call separation anxiety. The answer?

You gotta be kidding me.

CAT CHAT

BoBo
My owner's been gone for
four hours. Good.

SHOELACES

These short lengths of cotton, leather or synthetic fibres exist
for two reasons only.

Reason 1: a means for your owner to secure their footwear.
Reason 2: a special game for cats, the aim of which is to
untie them with your claws or teeth while your owner is
desperately trying to leave the house.

CAT CHAT

Georgie
The one thing
I really, really
hate in life …
double knots.

SHOES

Loafers, trainers, boots, stilettos, slippers, flip-flops, moccasins and sandals. An almost endless variety of textures and tastes … and all with a deliciously footy flavour. Chewing slowly on a well-worn slingback is like you've died and gone to kitty heaven. The problem, however, stems from humans' illogical attachment to shoes. Since we don't wear them, it's difficult to appreciate why they get so annoyed when we 'mutilate' their footwear. That's why, if you're going to chew a shoe, you must make sure you hide the evidence afterwards. Along with the other one of the pair.

CAT CHAT

L'il Minx
There's one thing better than shoes. Shoe boxes.

See also *Chewing*

SLEEPING

It's difficult to say accurately how long you should sleep, since there are lots of factors involved: your age, your breed, your health, your diet and your environment. And although the figures are different for each cat, you'll usually find you should sleep between twelve and sixteen hours a day. And the funny thing is that no matter how long we sleep, no one gives it a second thought. It's just accepted: 'Well, she's a cat and that's what cats do.'

For humans, though, it's completely different. If your owner were inactive for that length of time, it would be a sign that they were either a student or worked in local government.

CAT CHAT

Caboose
Why do we sleep so much? No one knows, and anyway, who cares? Just make the most of it.

See also *Catnap*

SPAYING

This section is for females. Toms should see *Neutering*. (Well, only if you don't mind being disturbed and upset.)

Spaying is the female version of neutering and although this involves surgery and a general anaesthetic, I have it on very good authority that it's easier to forget you had ovaries and a uterus than testicles.

Advantages of being spayed	Disadvantages of being spayed
• You won't go through heat cycles and the corresponding hormonal turmoil • You won't have to put up with unwanted attention from a whole host of randy male cats • And that's as much about not getting pregnant as it is not catching transmittable diseases • It reduces the likelihood of having breast cancer • You'll generally live a longer, healthier cat life	• You can't go outside for at least ten days after the operation. That means being subjected to at least ten days of daytime TV

SPRAY/SQUIRT BOTTLES/ WATER PISTOLS

More than dogs, more than small children that pet you too energetically and definitely more than cute babies that compete with you for attention, these insidious devices are your true enemy. Many books on so-called 'cat care' suggest that your owners should squirt or spray us with water as a means of training us and persuading us to stop what they see as 'bad habits'.

They call it a 'behavioural modification technique'. Our response: 'If you don't stop squirting me, I'll dig my claws into your flimsy human skin and you'll learn the true meaning of "negative reinforcement".

STAIRS

In addition to the one-step rule, when it comes to going downstairs ahead of your owner, make sure you remember to stop suddenly at random in order to lick yourself. This can be very amusing. For you, anyway.

See also *One-step rule, The*

STARING

For some reason a lot of people are uncomfortable around cats. Maybe it's our association with witches and witchcraft or the fact that we show a stealth-like quality as we move silently and eerily around the house. However, the number-one method to unsettle and creep out humans is to stare at them with such intensity and for such a long time that it seems like you're not just looking at them intently – **you are actually examining their very soul.**

2 WAYS TO CREEP OUT YOUR OWNERS EVEN MORE

1) Stare, but look past your owner at some invisible object just over their shoulder.
2) Run into the hall and suddenly stare at the front door (for enhanced effect, start hissing).
In both cases you must give the impression that you can definitely see something they can't. Something like a Victorian child.

CAT CHAT

Zoltar

Look into my eyes … Look into my eyes … You are feeling sleepy … but don't doze off before you bring me a second dinner.

See also *Glow-in the-dark-eyes*

STRANGERS

As a cat, you shouldn't get overly excited when anyone new comes into the house. Why react this way? It's highly doubtful that they're more important than you.

STYLING IT OUT

An important life lesson for a cat is to remember to make any mistake look intentional.

Whether it's misjudging that leap from the chair to the windowsill and plunging to the floor, or running into a room, skidding on laminate flooring and crashing head first into a table leg, just conceal your pain and shrug with an expression that says, 'Sure. Of course I meant to do that.' Remember, as a species, **we are far too proud to admit errors of judgement**.

SUN, LYING IN THE

Just because cats can't get suntans doesn't mean we don't love the sun. That's why, given half a chance, you'll find us warming ourselves in the hallway, by the open back door or on a patio.

However, the thing we like almost as much as the sun is the shade.

A typical way to spend a morning in the summer months

Step 1: Lie in sun
Step 2: Get too hot
Step 3: Find shade
Step 4: Get too cold
Step 5: Repeat Steps 1 to 4 until dinner time

N.B. A great way to get warm is by lying in the road. Not only does the dark surface really absorb the heat, making it nice and toasty, but it also enables us to give car drivers who slow down to avoid us a satisfying 'F you!' expression.

TAILS

Your fellow cats will understand and appreciate what we're feeling from the different movements of our tail, whether it's raised, raised with a slightly bent tip, swaying, swishing, lowered, bristled, swinging back and forth between your legs or curled around your body. They'll also recognize that the position of our bodies and even how we move our ears add subtlety to these messages.

Humans will not. They have absolutely no idea what each movement signifies and think we act the same way as dogs. Please. We're far more complicated creatures who display a host of nuances in every twitch. When a dog wags its tail, you generally know it's happy. When we do the same thing it can mean that we're feeling distress, frustration, aggression, agitation, curiosity or annoyance. Sometimes several of these emotions in quick succession.

Because of this confusion it's best to avoid relying on tail movements when you want to communicate with people and, instead, use tried and tested vocal methods.

Remember, a hiss is worth a thousand wags.

The 3 reasons humans think we have tails

1. To communicate various emotions
2. To provide balance when running and turning
3. To fan our pheromones

CAT CHAT

Mungo
Flattened ears and a raised tail. Do I mean 'I need attention. Please pet me,' or 'I'm angry and in a very scratchy mood'? It'll be fun seeing if you guess right.

See also *Meowing*

The 3 reasons we really have tails

1. Something to chase when we get bored
2. To knock delicate ornaments off high shelves
3. To thump loudly and forcefully against our owner's bedroom door at 5.30 a.m.

TELEVISION

Do you know how you can tell that your owner feels guilty about leaving you alone in the house for long periods of time? They leave the television on.

They make a big fuss about choosing the right station and adjusting the volume and brightness, but what they fail to appreciate is that we have **absolutely no interest** in watching TV when they're out, or even, for that matter, when they're in. The reason is simple. It's not because we have inferior colour vision or our feline brains process images at a different frame rate: it's just that there's absolutely nothing worth watching.

CAT CHAT

Marlow
570 channels and
nothing on …

TERRITORY

The whole concept of 'territory' isn't that difficult to understand. In simple terms it's the area you consider to be yours and yours alone. Well, I say yours alone, but the hard fact is that you usually have to share it with your owners and their immediate family. It's a thing that goes back to when we were domesticated by humans thousands and thousands of years ago. We helped protect their harvests from pesky rodents and they gave us food and shelter. Now we can't shake them off.

There are just two things you need to do with territory:
1. Mark it
2. Defend it from intruders

Intruders

These come in many shapes and forms. Outside it could be birds, squirrels or foxes, while inside it usually means strangers and strange animals (like your owner's friend's yappy Yorkshire terrier). If you fail to protect your territory from these interlopers, then as soon as your back is turned the trespasser is likely to steal not only your food, your water or your catnip-infused squeaky toy, but could also be sitting on your favourite chair (a crime so heinous it really doesn't bear thinking about).

2 THINGS TO REMEMBER ABOUT TERRITORY

1. In the feline world, territory doesn't just mean the house or garden. It can also extend to the driveway, the neighbour's garden, the garden three doors down, the road and even the surrounding streets.
2. The more territory you have, the harder it is to defend. Remember that when you decide to mark your turf as the entire length of the street, including the garages and small strip of shops.

See also *Marking your territory*

THUNDERSTORMS

One moment you're looking out of the window, wondering why the sky has gone dark, cursing the heavy rain that is preventing you going out, and the next thing you know there's an almighty loud BOOM! That must surely herald the end of the world, right? If you didn't want to poop before, then you do now. And you might already have done so ...

This is called thunder, and it is completely natural to exhibit some level of uneasiness at the noise. Some cats experience just a feeling of mild anxiety, while for others the effect is blind panic and absolute dread terror.

For most cats, though, it's the fear of the unknown that causes distress, so the first thing to do is to establish what thunder is and isn't.

WHAT THUNDER IS

A sonic shock wave caused by a lightning bolt.

WHAT THUNDER ISN'T

The hugest, most unbelievably massive dog in the whole world outside the house (far, far bigger than even Digby, the Biggest Dog in the World), barking at you at the top of his voice.

While thunder is obviously frightening, you can use this natural weather phenomenon to your advantage. Think of it as authorization to do all the things you're not allowed to do in the house. This includes running at breakneck speed from room to room knocking things over, scratching all the things you're not meant to, climbing the curtains, going into rooms you're not allowed to go into, chewing shoes and, of course, peeing or pooping outside the litter box.

Your owner will attribute any unusual bad behaviour to you being upset by the loud noise. Not only will you be forgiven, there's a good chance you'll probably be stroked and given a treat.

Stormy weather? Suddenly it doesn't seem that frightening.

CAT CHAT

Madge
Okay ... so I'm a scaredy cat.

See also *Fireworks*

TOILETS

Also known as the bathroom, this is a room in the house containing that thing that appears to be a big white chair filled with water. This is the place where your owners go to read the newspaper or play on their phones; it's also the place where they pee and poop. Think of it as a sort of high-tech litter box. For cats, though, the toilet provides the best opportunity to interact with humans. **It's the place to go and stare at them**.

CAT CHAT

Nero
Take my advice.
Stick with a litter tray.

See also *Bathrooms* and *Litter trays/Litter boxes*

TRAINING

Every so often your owner will try to train you to respond to basic commands. What they don't appreciate is that, unlike dogs, which are true pack animals that just want to please the 'leader', we're fiercely independent and have very little interest or inclination to actually work for praise or attention, let alone treats. Over time it *is* possible for a cat to recognize a series of simple commands; it's just that we choose not to.

Don't feel guilty about frustrating your owner this way. Just remember that you're a cat, not a performing monkey.

5 common commands humans try to teach us

Command	The cat's natural reaction
Come!	Why?
Stay!	No
Sit!	Says who?
Get down!	Yeah, right
Stop that!	Whatever

TREES

A book entitled *How to Be a Cat* without a section on trees is like having a book called *How to Be a Dog* (and I believe there is one) without a section on butt-sniffing. It's that integral to our whole being.

Sharpening our claws by sinking them into soft bark is marginally more satisfying than sharpening them on thick carpet, the side of an armchair or our owner's leg. But trees provide far more enjoyment than just letting us have a good, long, satisfying scratch without being yelled at. They provide a convenient way to get a better view of potential predators and prey – as well as providing a handy escape route from shouty dogs. When we're up a tree we're able to study our entire domain, lords of all we survey. Although, this isn't as grand as it sounds, because our domain usually includes the unkempt back garden, a rusty barbecue, a shed that's falling to bits and the neighbour's sludge-filled pond.

Still, sometimes it's nice to get away from it all.

If you get stuck

The lack of cat skeletons in trees is proof that all cats will eventually get down. The first thing to do is actually something *not* to do: panic.

The second thing to do is understand that there's a physiological reason you can't climb down a tree the way you climbed up it: head first. It's your claws. They curve inwards so you won't get any grip as you head down. But don't worry. There are three tried and tested ways to return to the ground:

1. Slowly, by descending tail first
2. Quickly, by jumping
3. Being rescued by what humans call the Fire Brigade

UNGRATEFUL, BEING

Displaying this characteristic should be key to how you live your life. It's essential in everything you do and it's what separates us from dogs. Give them a treat and they'll jump up and down or run in circles howling with delight. We, on the other hand, should just put on our best 'don't-give-a-crap' attitude.

When your owner interacts with you, under no circumstances must you show any degree of satisfaction, let alone acknowledgement.

Example:

1. Meow for food.
2. When your owner puts the bowl down, turn your nose up and walk away.*

*Of course, come back later when no one's looking.

URINE SPRAYING

Urine spraying isn't as straightforward as it seems. (Well, the act of spraying itself is easy – all you have to do is back up to an object, raise your tail and spray.) What I mean is that the reasons we spray aren't as clear-cut as just marking out our territory to tell other cats, 'Back off, pal. I was here first!' Think of spraying urine as a means of communicating what you're feeling. Okay, it may be less pleasant than meowing or purring, and it's definitely smellier, but it's still an important way to express yourself.

5 reasons why you might want to spray urine, apart from marking your territory

1. Because you're scared
2. Because you're anxious
3. Because you want to make an unfamiliar object familiar
4. Because you really, really hate that new couch
5. And the wallpaper

VACUUM CLEANERS

Letting your imagination run away with itself can cause great anxiety. Take, for example, that dark scary cave in the hall. That's just the cupboard under the stairs. And the evil monster that lives there? Well, that's something called a vacuum cleaner. It's a machine humans use to clean the house, a process that includes picking up your shed fur. And while vacuum cleaners can emit a loud roar like an evil monster and can be just as terrifying, the scary noise doesn't last for long.

You'll probably hear it about twice a week (more frequently if you moult a lot), although if you live with just a male human, you'll only hear the vacuum cleaner on very rare occasions.

VEGETABLES

With the completely misjudged notion that they should improve our nutrition, your owners might decide to supplement your normal diet with vegetables. The facts are as follows:

A. We don't need vegetables
B. We don't want vegetables

What's worse is that things like garlic, onions, chives, tomatoes and avocados can all be toxic to us. When it comes to your health, don't take any chances. **Avoid every vegetable**.

CAT CHAT

RicRoc
I thought I'd never find anything as bland and unexciting as dry cat food. Then I discovered vegetables.

VETS

Some vets are in their dream career. They devote their life to helping sick pets get better, there's a huge amount of job satisfaction and every day is different. If you have one of these vets you're lucky. Most of us are looked after by someone who's doing the job because they weren't clever enough to be a human doctor. They take this simmering resentment out on us, usually in the form of rough manhandling and a degree of prodding and poking usually associated with someone sorting fruit rather than anything connected with the medical profession.

And each time you're on their examination table, they're thinking, 'I could have been a world-leading neurosurgeon. Instead I'm examining this British longhair for mange.'

5 reasons we really don't like vets

1. They shame us by telling us we have worms
2. And that we're overweight
3. They're the ones who recommend the Cone of Shame
4. Three words: anal gland draining
5. One more word: vaccinations

A guide to what to expect at the vet

Waiting room
This is where we're imprisoned in our cat carriers and get barked at by stupid dogs.

Reception desk
This gives the impression you're at a swish hotel that prides

itself on providing outstanding comfort for its customers. Nothing could be further from the truth.

The scales
These exist just so the vet can tut and then sell your owner expensive diet cat food.

The examination table
Stainless-steel surface that offers three things: a cold surface for your bottom, zero grip and a potentially painful drop on to a hard floor.

X-Ray room
If you've swallowed something you shouldn't have, this is the place to find out. Keys, screws, stones, small toys, bones, Lego men, computer mice, jewellery, crayons, batteries, USB sticks and elastic bands. In this room, the truth will always prevail.

Operating theatre
The stuff that kitty nightmares are made of: bright lights, bizarre machines with tubes, lots of sharp things and people wearing masks.

Kennels
This is where animals are placed after an operation but before they're ready to go home. Don't let the name mislead you, though. They're not small wooden animal houses with pitched roofs, but stark metal cages. And, as you will inevitably discover, they are not just for dogs.

CAT CHAT

Bertie

Vets? They're the people who'll remove not just a thorn from your paw, but also your testicles.

WAKING HUMANS

You might be hungry, you might be cold or you might want to wake your owner up just for the hell of it. It's not important. What does matter is that you learn the multitude of ways to do so. Of course, it's acceptable to stick with one tried and tested method you know works, but then you risk the danger of your owners becoming immune to it. (Okay, I know it's difficult to imagine that anyone could reach a stage where they manage to ignore you wailing like a ghoul mere inches from their ear, but it could happen.) So, with that in mind, here are some options for you to try.

The 15 most effective ways to wake your owner from a deep, satisfying sleep

1. Relentlessly scratch the side of the bed, chair or couch.
2. Lie under the bed on your back and slowly pull yourself along with your claws.
3. Drag your claws ever so slowly and screechingly across the dressing room mirror.
4. Position yourself two inches from their ear. Start with a gentle meow and escalate this into a banshee wail.
5. Knead their face with your paws.
6. Energetically lick their nose, ears or lips with your rough tongue.
7. Go for a gentle stroll all over their body.
8. Leap from an adjoining piece of furniture or surface directly on to their stomach or back.
9. Walk round and round in circles on top of the duvet.
10. Repeatedly tap their chin with your paw (this is considered very subtle … and, as such, is really no fun at all).
11. Present your bottom to their face (only if they have a good sense of smell).
12. Sit on their chest and stare.
13. Try and lift their eyelids to see if they're really asleep, rather than just faking it.
14. Climb under the duvet and worm your way up using your claws on the bedding and your owner in order to get purchase.
15. Sit on the bedside table and systematically swipe things on to the floor, such as their watch, earrings, wallet, change, receipts etc., one item at a time.

If all else fails

Scratch them. (You'll know they're fully awake when they shout, 'Not the face! Not the face!')

See also *Bladder*

WALKIES

Do we look like dogs, sound like dogs or act like dogs? No? Then don't take us for walks!

Unless you live in Paris and your owner is an old lady or a particularly stylish man, then there is absolutely no need to attach a lead to our collar and take us around the streets. If you do, you'll look like an idiot.

Worse still, so will we.

WARM SPOT

The warm spot is the area immediately under where your owner is sitting; it could be a chair, a couch or the bed. **As a human, it's their job to create the warm spot; as a cat, it's your duty to take it**. Essentially, your mission to take the warm spot must be undertaken like a police stake-out. As such, its success will rely on three things.

Stay alert

You might be watching and anticipating the warm spot for half an hour or more. Longer if your owner has good bladder control or is really engaged with the television show he's watching. Although it's tempting to go to sleep rather than wait, stay focused and fight any temptation to doze off: the window of opportunity to take the warm spot might only be a matter of seconds. If you're dreaming of chasing mice you'll miss it. You snooze, you lose.

Plan ahead

When it comes to taking the warm spot successfully, forward planning is everything. You'll need to decide where to position yourself, when to make your move and also what to do if the mission is compromised. You'll need to be able to think the whole process out from beginning to end and deal with unexpected changes to the plan (like your owner deciding not to make a cup of tea during a commercial break).

Speed is everything

Your optimum position will be a careful balance of a location that gives you a good vantage point for surveillance, but also that's within easy leaping distance of the warm spot when the time comes. As soon as your owner momentarily gets up or goes out of the room, make your move with pace and purpose. He who hesitates is not only lost, but also destined to spend the rest of the evening on the floor.

> ## WHEN YOU EVENTUALLY TAKE THE WARM SPOT
>
> Stretch out, close your eyes and pretend to be asleep. If anyone pokes you or tries to move you, show your claws and hiss.

WASHING MACHINES

The first time you see a washing machine in operation it might seem fascinating and even hypnotizing. There's the mysterious low rumble, the mesmerizing sound of water and the pulsating bright lights. Don't waste your time staring at it because this is all you'll ever see:

- Human clothes going round one way
- Human clothes going round the other way

This is as good as it gets.

CAT CHAT

Chow
Will it get my whites whiter?

See also *Hiding places*

WATER

Water to cats is like water to the Wicked Witch of the West. You'd think that being as fastidious as we are with grooming we'd love water, but you'd be wrong. Very wrong. Humans who try to put us into a bath usually learn about our hatred of water the hard way, and what starts off as a well-intentioned attempt to get us clean ends up with them spending the rest of the evening dabbing scratched hands and arms with antiseptic.

Why don't we take to water? Humans have claimed that it's down to evolution: that we associate water with water-based predators (even lions are scared of crocodiles), or the fact that a damp smell can alert prey to our presence. The real reason? In human terms, it's the equivalent of having to sit in wet clothes.

See also *Baths*

WINDOW BLINDS

Like the inside of washing machines or dryers, neighbours' garden sheds and open fires, window blinds are NOT YOUR FRIEND. Sure, they look innocent enough – thin, horizontal slats separating you from an unhindered view of outside – but they're the window-dressing equivalent of the Venus flytrap. One false move and you're caught tight, and even if you manage to extract yourself before your owners return home, it's unlikely you'll be able to conceal the evidence of your wrongdoing.

CAT CHAT

Pussy Willow
I knew they should have bought curtains.

WITCHCRAFT

Are you sure you're a cat? Yes, you may look like one, but the thing is, you may not be …

Now, I know that sounds like the ramblings of a mad

moggy, but those who believe in witchcraft consider cats to be animal-shaped spirits called 'familiars', whose job is to serve a witch, helping her in casting spells and generally acting as her companion. Most familiars are called things like Salem, Pyewocket or Crookshanks and are short-haired black or ginger cats; tabbies don't really look 'otherworldly', and if you're white and fluffy … well, no one's going to be intimidated by you, are they?

A sure sign that you are indeed a familiar is the fact that you possess supernatural powers. The ability to leap to the top of a garden fence in a single bound or haul yourself along a washing line are examples of your innate agility, not any form of magic. Of course, these powers could be lying dormant, which is why it's important to know if your owner is, in fact, a witch.

7 sure-fire signs that your owner might actually be a witch

- Her Facebook identity is Woodsprite or Moondaughter
- She prefers the Vernal Equinox to Christmas
- She runs around woodland at night naked
- She cooks in a cauldron rather than a Le Creuset casserole dish
- Halloween is viewed as a religious holiday, not a commercial travesty
- She spells the word magic with a 'k' on the end
- She has a bumper sticker that reads: 'My other car is a broomstick'

WOOL/YARN

Forget intricate cat towers or tunnels. Some of the most fun playthings are the simplest – and you can't get simpler than a ball of wool. I mean, all it is is a ball of wool!

Humans use wool (or yarn, as it's sometimes called) to make clothes, or if they really have no excitement in their lives, teapot covers. 'Knitting', as they call it, is sadly not as fashionable as it once was. If you are fortunate to live in a household where your owner does knit, then you'll have a ball (literally). Yet, while there's great fun to be had in batting the wool around the floor like an injured mouse or tangling it around things, here are a few words of advice.

Wool dos and don'ts

- DO try and locate your owner's sewing box, or as this mythical place is known to cats, Yarnia
- DON'T eat the wool. It is a textile fibre, not spaghetti
- DON'T play with acrylic yarn. We have standards!
- DO knock balls of wool from your owner's lap as she knits
- DON'T get excited if you hear your owner talking about string theory. She is not hypothesizing about how to entertain you; it's something very dull to do with gravity and the fundamental structure of our universe

There is no truth to the rumour that if you play with wool when you're pregnant you'll give birth to mittens.

CAT CHAT

Felix
My owners know I like wool, but this time they went too far.

WORMS

You know that nice warm, fuzzy feeling inside of you? That's a sign that you're content. On the other hand, you know that feeling of lethargy and hunger combined with chronic diarrhoea? That's probably worms.

Treatment for these parasites is widely available in the form of liquids, tablets or, god forbid, injections. If you do suffer from worms, the thing that hurts most isn't the discomfort to your stomach, it's the damage to your social standing.

YOGA FOR CATS

Cats don't have frustrating commutes, annoying bosses, money problems, unruly children, volatile relationships – or any one of the hundreds of reasons humans get stressed out. Unfortunately for us, though, some humans have taken to involving us in their de-stressing methods. What I'm talking about is being dragged along to cat yoga sessions.

I know this sounds ludicrous, but I'm not joking. Cat yoga is a 'thing'. A thing that ironically causes *us* stress. We just want to be at home, curled up somewhere warm and cosy, not in a draughty hall surrounded by a load of pretentious ladies who lunch called Arabella or Tamara, stretching and bending while we wander round aimlessly, waiting to go home. They've been told (and they believe it!) that being surrounded by cats will help them relax and achieve a higher state of consciousness. They also claim that our presence helps bonding and nurtures our 'cat karma'.

Now I don't know about you, but I'd rather spend time licking my genitals than cleansing my chakra. Cat yoga? As dogs would say, 'That's just barking!'

CAT CHAT

Trixie
Do I look
like this is relaxing
me?

THE END